Happiness-Based Mindfulness

An Exploration of Happiness-Based Mindfulness
Approaches and a practical application of the concepts from
the book *You Are Love: The Discovery of Happiness*

Sara Spowart, PHD, DMFT, LMFT, MPA, MA

Author's Note

I wanted to create a mental health psychoeducation program that could be applied practically, in an easy-to-replicate way, to help almost anyone, and provide concrete tools from my book "You Are Love: The Discovery of Happiness." Happiness-Based Mindfulness and the accompanying literature in this book are the result of this endeavor. In this book I review Happiness-Based Mindfulness as well as the background and information on the reason and logic for the activities. This program is provided in five proposed formats. These include a one hour workshop, 3 session trauma-based format, a version for youth, a general 6-week version and an in-depth intensive 12-week format. This book, like my book "You Are Love: The Discovery of Happiness," is the representation of my hope to provide information in a practical, feasible way to sustainably improve happiness for anyone that uses it.

Wishing you happiness, joy, peace, love, kindness, and the experience of being complete<3

"May all beings be happy. May all beings feel love. May all beings know the truth of their own nature. May all beings be free."

Introduction

This book is a culmination of lessons I've realized and I hope will be of support and help to many. When I was a child, there was a necklace I asked my mom to buy, it had a pendant on it that said "May all beings be happy. May all beings feel love. May all beings know the truth of their own nature. May all beings be free." Our feeling of freedom is innately tied to our happiness, ability to love, and knowing of our own inner nature. When we realize, and activate our own true nature, by default we experience happiness, love, peace and freedom. When we know we can conjure these things ourselves, without reliance on the outside, that alone is freedom. So how do we conjure these emotions? How do we become our own conscious creator of emotions? Well, we've always been our own 'conjurer' of emotions and energy, but we didn't know it. When we are reacting to our environment, our experiences, our thoughts, perceptions and view of reality…this is a 'conjuring' of emotion. This reaction to the outside is our own creation of energy, of emotion. Emotion can be seen as energy in motion.

When we master our emotions, we master our energy and can create our inner experience largely how we want to. We are able to independently determine our inner state to some degree at this point. This is in contrast to living in a reactive state to perceived circumstances or life events. Something I use with clients is an emotion chart I made that divides up emotions into five zones. This chart is a mindfulness tool and also helps create awareness of cycles we may be unknowingly caught in as well as more of a focus on state of being, versus life events and circumstances for creating more happiness. It is also based in the theory that 'what we measure, we improve.' Therefore, by 'measuring' or taking notice of our emotional experiences every day, it creates more detachment from the emotions or cycles you may feel stuck in. It also helps create greater awareness of the state of being you'd prefer and focus more on that.

In the Emotion Chart, there is the 'Red Zone' or destructive/cyclical emotions; the 'Green Zone' or relief/somewhat positive emotions; the 'Blue Zone' which are uplifting and energizing emotions; the 'Purple Zone' which are considered freedom or stabilizing emotional experiences; and lastly the 'Yellow Zone' for transcendence and the realization that you have gone beyond painful reactions to prior issues. Like selecting a food item on a menu, we can work backwards, as an observer, not a reactor to life…and choose the state of being we would like to exist in. This may seem like an abstract concept, but it is possible to choose your state of being and have that be your normal everyday experience of how you feel. You can go from reacting and living largely in the 'Red Zone' of the emotion chart, to abiding and living in the 'Blue Zone' or focusing on the 'Purple Zone' most, if not all the time. We are human beings because we exist in a certain *state of being*, in the physical form of a human.

So, if you could **choose your state of being**, what 'state' would you choose??

What Is The Goal of Happiness-Based Mindfulness Mean?

Focusing on creating the emotion you would like to experience more, is the fastest way I have found to create the state of being you'd like to experience. Below is the emotion chart I made with the red, green, blue, purple, and yellow zones. Checking in with yourself every day can be helpful for not only creating awareness but also for reducing destructive and painful emotions, and increasing positive emotions. What we notice, we improve. This is true for all aspects of life, including things like diet, exercise, sleep, relationships, financial habits, health habits, etc. When we cultivate an increased 'reflective capacity' through practicing awareness, noticing where we are on the emotion chart, and regular mindfulness practices, we can begin to feel happier and happier by changing and altering things that are causing pain and problems, as well as bring more love and positive emotion into our lives. Even if it is painful at first to bring awareness to your life, by practicing this awareness, you can start to see what 'zone' you are living in most of the time. Are you in the 'Red Zone,' 'Green Zone,' 'Blue Zone' most of the time? The 'Purple Zone' is after the 'Blue Zone' and can help bring more stabilization of happiness and well-being that is cultivated. The Purple Zone and Blue Zones are also very powerful for getting out of the Red Zone in a sustainable way.

It may seem to some that this is a very self-centered approach and all about the self. However, that is where we have to start. Also, the reality about suffering is if we can't get our own suffering under control, it will by default eventually spill out and hurt ourselves and others. The best protector for yourself and others is to have some intention and mastery over your state of being. Have you ever been in a room and someone with a lot of anxiety, anger or depression walks in? Even if you are not a highly sensitive person, you will be able to eventually feel the impact of it. This may be that you can feel the suffering yourself, or it may be that the suffering person is unkind and toxic in some way to you or others. However, their suffering will eventually be felt. Conversely, have you ever had the experience of meeting someone who is incredibly peaceful, loving or compassionate? Their kindness and positive emotion will also flow out and positively impact you too. We are all inter-connected. Therefore, mastering or having some intentional awareness around your state of being is one of the most loving, brave and kindest things you can do for yourself and others. Our state of being matters and has a ripple effect on ourselves, others, our family, relationships, pets, our environment and maybe more.

I will tell you a secret, or little-known outcome of all of this…it's love. At the end, when we get beyond the Red Zone and into greater and greater states of positivity, you will find that you are on a path where the ego falls more and more away, and your sense of love for yourself and others naturally grows. In fact, there is a tipping point with insights, at which you just continue to increase positivity and love in everything and everywhere. Dropping to lower states of being becomes an unnatural and uncomfortable feeling, and feeling positive and happy becomes your new normal. Ultimately, it all leads down a road to greater and greater love until finally your love spreads out further and further, and has no boundaries. This is a truly liberating state to be in, when you can and do love everyone and everything. Loving at this capacity does not mean that you accept and embrace everything everywhere. It does not mean you align or approve of violence, negativity, poverty, abuse, and any other forms of negativity you are exposed to or considering. However, it does mean that you have unconditional, compassionate love and are able to place that unconditional, compassionate love in any direction you choose.

There is something called an 'Object Love' meditation that can be helpful for practicing this. With this type of meditation, you are taking the concept of loving-kindness or Metta meditation and expanding it to include inanimate objects or creatures. This could be practicing feeling love for buildings, nature, countries, homes, pets, bank accounts, etc. It is a deepening of the practice of unconditional love and the idea that love comes from you, as the source, and to not look to the outside to receive the love and kindness you want and hope for. The key to 'loving all' is to learn and understand that you yourself, are a channel or source of love. Certain things can inspire love to pour through and from you, but that energy is still coming *from* you.

Similarly, when you experience hate, the hate is coming from you. That is not to say you have not been harmed by someone, but rather that the source of the emotion comes from you. The highest levels of happiness I have encountered thus far come from, in part, being in the flow state of loving others, loving expansively, or just loving for no reason at all. Some of the happiest individuals (and very rare individuals) I have encountered, have a sense of inherent love that stems from them and flows outward. They are able to love strangers, animals, objects, God, people that have wronged them, and really anyone and anything. They do this because they understand this is a powerful form of living they can embody. Even if life has been tremendously hard for them, they still love. Even if there seems to be no reason at all to feel anything but hurt and pain or hatred, they still love. Even if they've experienced horrific prejudice, poverty, rejection, and suffering, they still love. No matter what, they don't react to things around them, and they maintain some state of love. They do this, if anything, out of love for themselves because they don't want to harm themselves or add to any suffering more than what has already occurred.

In large part, it is a choice. Loving all and loving on an expansive level is a choice and commitment. It is not necessarily easy and does not mean that it won't be challenged, but it is the best way I have seen to be happy in a sustainable way and to varying degrees. When we love with unconditional compassion, we go beyond ourselves and our limited perspectives, viewpoints, and habits. We rise above limitations and the contradictions that life presents, and we provide another alternative. When we are abused, we can love. When we are disappointed and feel hopeless, we can love. When we are exhausted, we can love. When we feel isolated, alone, or lost, we can love. When we are being consumed in fear and self-preservation, we can love. When we are being narcissistic or self-absorbed, we can love. When we have an addiction, or we are looking to the outside for satiation, we can love. We can love no matter what is occurring on the outside, and it will serve as a protective factor against anything that may be experienced. We can love, by focusing on the state of love, the experience of love. We can practice love, regardless of what is occurring around us.

A key component of Happiness-Based Mindfulness is built on the idea that each step builds on the other. We build step by step to higher levels of well-being, while still maintaining unconditional compassion for more destructive/painful emotions. There are five versions presented here. The first version looks at the general 6-week program, the second version is the 12-week in-depth approach, the third version looks at a brief trauma-focused approach, the fourth version is to help support children and youth, and the fifth version is a 1-hour workshop that can be easily replicated and implemented. All five versions have the same end goal, which is to meet participants where they are at and provide basic building block tools to increase your happiness no matter where you are at.

Become What You Want to See in The World

What do you want to see in the world?

A common issue I have experienced, and I've seen everyone experience for the most part, is the idea that 'you can't be happy', because of unwanted things that may be happening. Often, the outer reality does not reflect the world we want to experience. However, just because the outer reflection may look a certain way, this doesn't mean we do not have the power to do something constructive about it. As we are all so intricately interconnected, when we change ourselves, it has a ripple effect that goes out and impacts far beyond what we know or see. Therefore, instead of looking outward with a reactive mentality, what if we see ourselves as little energy beings that can direct our energy how we want, and in an intentional way.

For example, if you want to have more love in your life, you can imagine that you are radiating out love from yourself to others, and you can be intentionally loving and kind to others. You can give love in whatever form you imagine every day. By giving love, that energy of love will come through you and you will also experience it yourself. This will also attract and bring more love into your love, as you become a more and more loving person. To bring in peace, the same thing. Act with intention to bring more peace every day and in any small way you can think of. The experience of peace that is coming through you… will help *you* to feel more peaceful, bring peace back to you, and create greater levels of peace around you. This philosophy can be applied to nearly any situation.

However, don't give love or peace with the intention of it coming back to you or an expectation of having something in return. This cancels out the positive. The intention needs to be as pure as possible. Give for the sake of giving. Provide peace to others or something outside of yourself for the sake of peace, and love for the sake of love. Detach from the expectation of an outcome or trying to manipulate reality to have the outcome you want. You can have some power over this, and it will help you to feel happier, more present, and mindful no matter what the situation. Don't wait to feel good to do positive behaviors; just start from where you are now and it will create a new momentum and cycle of creation.

Main Components from The Book
You Are Love: The Discovery of Happiness

I wrote another book titled; You Are Love: The Discovery of Happiness. In this book, I talk about the realization of the power we have inside of ourselves to create the emotions and connections we search for. I also discuss four stages of realization that lead to understanding that we ourselves are love. These include the idea of the 1) Victim Stage where you may feel you are the victim of yourself, circumstances or outside people. In this stage we tend to look to the outside to fix things. We may look to be saved, or for a hero or something to fix everything. Or we might feel in a state of blame for everything, and looking outside of ourselves or at ourselves to blame for everything that 'has gone wrong.' The issue with the Victim Stage, and any angle you take it, is that it's incredibly self-centered. Although outside things or changes in ourselves can positively impact our situation temporarily, it is ultimately not the solution to being free from this cycle of perception. It is self-centered because it revolves around trying to alleviate your own experience of pain, as the solution to everything. It is also a lens from which to view the world. Ultimately it is unsatisfying and you can become trapped in a cycle of victim-hood that goes around and around. The diagram below provides a breakdown and overview of this stage with a visual cycle.

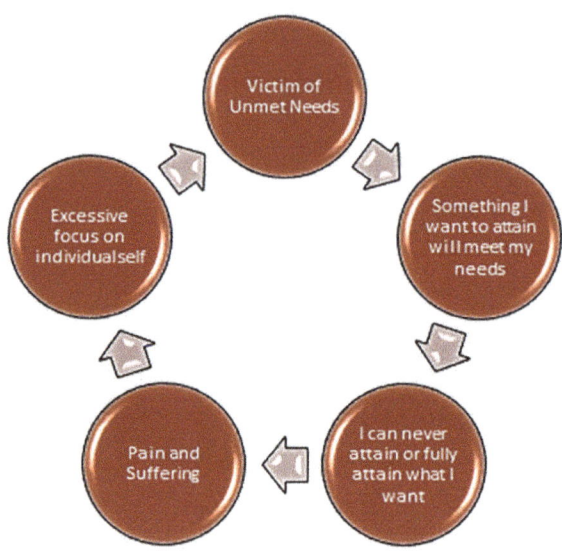

The cycle begins to end when the individual starts to wake up at some point and realize that there is more to happiness and well-being than the grasping, clinging or pushing away of what they want or don't want. Also, when there is a realization that there are many people, not just them and many perspectives and a larger picture are happening than just what is impacting their individual life. Someone can suffer a lot by worrying about others in their life and how they are doing, but it is still that the individual is placing their own beliefs of how things 'should' be going for others and they are suffering do to their own beliefs, instead of abiding in what is, and living non-judgmentally or with love. Fear is a strong emotion in the Victim Stage.

After the Victim Stage is the Giving Stage, in this stage there is no longer the focus on the individual self and suffering. The perspective widens to become more of a larger, bird's eye view. There is more of a system's understanding and systems approach. The ego falls away and is no longer the stronghold of one's life and existence. There is a sense of wanting to give and a belief and understanding that somehow there is more than enough to give wherever you can. Instead of a 'taking' approach to life, there is a creative and giving approach. In this stage, there is the effort of creating and building things in order to contribute. You see your own ability to create and give, and not that you are in a state of constant lack and a need to take whatever you can get. The Giving Stage is very empowering, love-filled and energetic.

The next two stages after this in the book You Are Love: The Discovery of Happiness are the Shifting Stage and the Infinity Stage. In the Shifting Stage, the concept of the self, changes more. The more you give to others in the giving stage, the less there seems to be a "me" and "you," and the more you can feel the interconnection between yourself and others. During the transition between the giving and shifting stages, you may start to see yourself in others. You begin to feel less that there is a "you" and "others," and more that others are part of you and you are part of them. Giving to another becomes the same as giving to yourself. During the transition into the shifting stage, your sense of self shifts. You start to see that you are not just "you." In the Infinity Stage you go beyond the experience of the Shifting Stage and may experience all of life as a flow, a stream of energy. The experience of this flow can come sooner, but it has greater significance from different perspectives. Eventually, it shifts so you become the flow itself and openness itself. Becoming the flow itself means there is an energy that flows through you and picks up speed. The ego and the concept of 'you' and 'I' falls away because it is no longer needed, and there is a sense of living in a stream and flow that is endless and everything.

The overview of these four stages are shortened to provide background information for the contents of this particular book. From the book "You Are Love: The Discovery of Happiness," the Happiness-Based Mindfulness approach was born. Included here are five approaches to practically apply, in concrete terms, exercises, approaches and interventions to get yourself out of the Victim Stage and into the Giving Stage, and potentially higher. A 1–2 hour workshop, a Youth-Focused Approach, A Trauma-Focused Approach, A 6-week General Approach and a 12-Week in-depth approach are all provided. In a way, you can think of these like a mental health improvement bootcamp with various levels of intensity, commitment and effort required. All of these approaches require effort and work. You have to want to feel better and be willing to do the work to change your inner state and perspective. However, I have used these approaches with thousands of clients and in general, have seen consistently incredible, positive results. I believe the overwhelmingly positive results I see in my therapy and life coaching work are due to my consistent and intuitive application of the tools I created in this book. However, it is also due to the level of desire of each individual to feel better. Working to improve our happiness is a selfless act, as well as an act of self-love. When we feel better, we create a positive ripple effect on everything around us. I hope these tools and the Happiness-Based Mindfulness approach brings you some comfort, hope, and a solid basis from which to improve your inner state of being and overall happiness ☺

Central Component of Happiness-Based Mindfulness: The Emotion Chart

One of the most important aspects of the Happiness-Based Mindfulness approach is the Emotion Chart. This is a mindfulness tool that helps you to become aware of the cycles of emotion you are caught in, and also to decide which emotions you'd like to experience and baby steps to get there. It is comprised of the red, green, blue, purple and yellow zones. A diagram of the full chart is provided below.

PURPLE ZONE: FREEDOM EMOTIONS

Unity, Big Picture Perspective, Integration, Freedom From 'Self', Seeing 'Self' in 'Other'

Compassion-Based Giving, Balance between 'Self' and 'Other,' Authenticity, Service, Creativity, Imagination, Faith, Inter-Dependence, Vision, Empowerment

Purpose, Meaning, Mission, Flow State, Connection, Truth, Beauty, Goals, Wisdom

BLUE ZONE: UPLIFTING & LIGHTENING EMOTIONS

*Bliss, Serenity, Peace, Harmony, Self-Awareness, Balance
Joy, Enthusiasm, Abundance, Exhilaration, Hope*

*Compassion, Empathy, Inspiration, Clarity, Presence
Love, Appreciation, Gratitude, Devotion, Generosity*

GREEN ZONE: RELIEF EMOTIONS

*Cooperation, Trust, Letting Go, Detachment
Satisfaction, Amusement, Curiosity*

*Power, Strength, Agency, Discovery, Challenge, Discipline
Self-Esteem, Dignity, Duty, Obligation
Neutral, Acceptance, Contentment, Safety
Happy, Excited, Surprised, Fun*

RED ZONE: DESTRUCTIVE & CYCLICAL EMOTIONS

*Anxiety, Nervousness, Shock, Confusion, Control, Stressed, Co-Dependent
Anger, Rage, Avoidance
Guilt, Resentment
Fear, Hatred, Blame, Denial, Self-Centeredness
Sadness, Grief, Loss*

*Isolated, Disconnected, Lonely, Duality
Hopelessness, Resignation, Depression
Powerlessness, Overwhelm, Frozen, Terror, Trauma
Shame, Apathy, Helplessness*

From this chart, imagine you are a ball of energy and are reacting to some challenging emotions or experiences. Let's say your reactions are causing you to be in the Red Zone. The first step here is to see, as an *observer*, not a reactor, that you are in the Red Zone. Then decide if you want to stay in the Red Zone or not. In general, what I have seen is the more we love ourselves and others, the less we will tolerate staying in or empowering, the red zone if there is any way we can change it. If you'd like to be in the green or blue zone, practicing loving self-awareness is a fast way to get there. In terms of steps:

1. **first practice being an observer instead of a reactor,**
2. **identify and come to an understanding of what emotion zone/s you tend to exist in (red,green, blue),**
3. **learn the patterns and beliefs that are keeping you in the emotional zone you don't prefer,**
4. **choose the zone you want to live in most of the time,**
5. **do the baby steps or steps to practice the emotions and zone you prefer to be in**

However, there is a balance in this practice. From a certain state of consciousness, telling yourself or suggesting to someone else that they should decide to be happy, may be experienced as invalidating and insulting their current state of pain and difficulty. Therefore, it is better and more effective to meet someone else *where they are at,* or the emotional zone they predominately are in. We are *not* our reactions; we are actually the experiencers and observers of these reactions. From that place of detachment, we can more easily move to the zone or emotional range we prefer to be in.

Yet that being said, the 'Red Zone' has very sticky, dense, heavy, and low emotions. Once you get into the 'red zone' it can be tough to get out. By its very nature, the emotions in the red zone help to keep you there and to grow and increase the negative emotions. For example, anger and angry outbursts tend to create more anger, sadness tends to create more sadness, anxiety tends to create more anxiety, and so on. What does this mean? It means that reacting to our negative emotions may help release the emotions and be cathartic. But, more often than not, the habitual reaction over and over again, actually helps to create patterns, habits, and neural pathways that make certain reactions and experiences more automatic and 'normal' and get us more stuck. There is an art to 1) allowing the Red Zone, and painful emotions to arise, 2) noticing them and 3) then letting them go with love.

Foundational Components of Happiness-Based Mindfulness: *The Destructive Painful 'Red' Zone*

Within the Emotion Chart, there are numerous components, and they come together in a way that can be easily understood for emotional regulation, support, and management. Specifically, in the Emotion Chart, the Red Zone is categorized, per the Happiness-Based Mindfulness approach, as going from lowest to highest emotions. Shame, apathy, and helplessness are experienced as existing at the lowest end and then go upward from there, with anxiety, nervousness, stress, etc. existing at the 'best feeling' end of the spectrum. The general idea of the *Red Zone* emotions is that they tend to be heavy, sticky, a cyclical. They do not lend themselves towards clear seeing and thinking, and they tend to reinforce themselves in an ongoing loop that is very hard to get out of without self-awareness and detachment. The Emotion Chart itself is an opportunity to create awareness, mindfulness and detachment from the Red Zone itself. By observing the categories of the Emotion Chart through detachment and checking in on where you are at, this alone creates separation from the Red Zone. The Red Zone thrives on unconsciousness and lack of awareness. By being able to see the Red Zone emotions, and that you are in a cycle of the Red Zone, that in itself gets you out.

It thrives on reactivity and unconsciousness. Just by measuring and observing on a regular basis, you improve and shift the pattern.

Another aspect of the Red Zone is that it tends to unconsciously, and reactively 'improve' itself. Specifically, if you are experiencing Red Zone emotions such as shame, apathy or helplessness at the very bottom of the Red Zone, the unconscious reaction could be to try to improve the emotion or temporarily get out of the Red Zone. This may mean becoming angry, or having hatred, or focusing on stress or anxiety in order to not feel shame, powerlessness or hopelessness. According to the Happiness-Based Mindfulness approach, it feels better to have anxiety or anger, than shame and trauma. It feels better to have fear and hatred than apathy or terror, and so on. The idea is that we are continuously trying to feel better and improve our state of well-being, even if it's unconsciously and reactively. Yet, within the Happiness-Based Mindfulness approach, by cultivating awareness of our state of being, we can counter-balance it and escape the loop and cycle of unconscious, Red Zone, reactivity. The Red Zone chart and the Red Zone loop and cycle of destruction is provided below for a visual aid, example and demonstration of the challenges inherent in the Red Zone. However, just by noticing and checking on where you are every day, you get out of the Red Zone and reduce the reactive, unconscious patterns that keep you in there.

Red Zone Loop & Cycle of Destruction

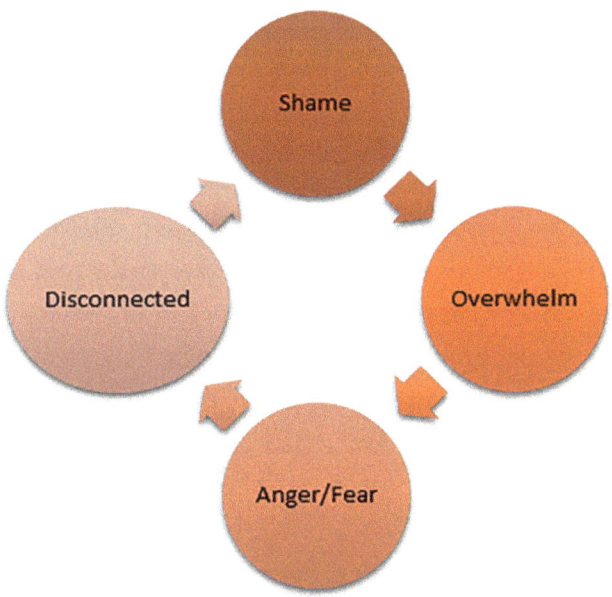

Foundational Components of Happiness-Based Mindfulness: *The Relief 'Green' Zone*

The next area up from the Red Zone is the Green Zone. The Green Zone is termed as Relief Emotions, because they provide relief from the pain of the Red Zone, or because they are used to provide temporary relief from the Red Zone. For example, some people become emotionally or verbally abusive because it provides them temporarily 'relief' from feeling powerless or shame in the Red Zone, to a short-lived experience of power, strength, self-esteem and safety in the Green Zone. Unfortunately, is is a destructive pattern and results in eventually dropping back down into the Red Zone and feeling even more shame, helplessness or other negative emotions as a result. There are positive and healthy ways to get into the Green Zone and experience relief, and there are negative, unhealthy and destructive ways to experience temporary relief. A healthy way to experience a shift from the Red Zone to the Green Zone might be to do work on affirmations, healing your shame, making amends, doing things to increase your self-esteem more authentically and in a more sustainable way. However, the healthier and more sustainable methods of going from the Red Zone to the Green Zone generally require more effort, continual practice and awareness. The unhealthy ways to increase from Red Zone to Green Zone tend to be fast, but unsustainable, and destructive and result in higher Red Zone levels later.

The Green Zone is termed the "Relief Emotions" because it provides respite and a break from painful or destructive emotions. Also, in the Green Zone you may feel lighter, have the ability to understand life patterns more clearly and make changes that would be much harder to do while in the Red Zone. The Green Zone also provides a solid base and good space from which to build positive emotions and actions on. Once in the Green Zone, it can be easier to build yourself and your life up to then go into the Blue Zone, Purple Zone or into the Yellow Zone of 'transcending' or going beyond issues. Individuals don't' generally feel stuck in the Green Zone, but they may feel there is eventually more to life that they would like to experience, or being in the Green Zone may be fragile or easily affected by other things. However, it is very different from the Red Zone where individuals are differing greatly and trying to find ways to have relief. In the Green Zone, there is relief and a feeling of safety and ease. There can be a sense or knowing that there is more, but there is also a relief from the pain that was experienced previously. From what I've seen in my clinical practice, most individuals seem to spend the majority of their time stuck in the Red Zone and unconscious, or do not know, how to get out. The Green Zone in theory also have a sense of bottom to top with the bottom emotions like 'fun' being less positive than the upper emotions of 'trust' and 'letting go,' however not necessarily. There can be overlap between fun and letting go for example or trust and fun. They can blend together in a positive, and constructive way. Instead of bottom to top, or cyclical, the Green Zone may be better understood a positively blended and the positive emotions can co-exist together. The diagram below with the circles and two-way arrow demonstrates this concept below. The Green Zone has blended and overlapping, positive emotions. There is not the sense of being stuck or trapped necessarily like in the Red Zone, but there is a sense of relief, but possibly a knowing that there is still more and not quite understanding how to get there.

GREEN ZONE: RELIEF EMOTIONS
*Cooperation, Trust, Letting Go, Detachment
Satisfaction, Amusement, Curiosity*

*Power, Strength, Agency, Discovery, Challenge, Discipline
Self-Esteem, Dignity, Duty, Obligation
Neutral, Acceptance, Contentment, Safety
Happy, Excited, Surprised, Fun*

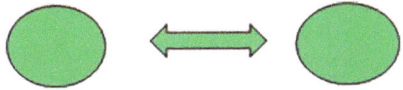

Foundational Components of Happiness-Based Mindfulness:
The Expansive 'Blue' Zone

The next area of the Emotion Chart after Green Zone is Blue Zone. Blue Zone is a special aspects of the Emotion Chart because within Blue Zone you also have the ability to get out of Red Zone and be freed from Red Zone cycles. Also, Blue Zone emotions are very constructive and powerful for creating new and positive things. Green Zone emotions are also powerful for creating something new, but Blue Zone is a new space to be. Blue Zone emotions may be found when someone falls in love, or has a child they care for, or a near death experience and new appreciation for the world, or practicing mindfulness every day and greater balance and self-awareness. It is a different level than Green Zone and also has the ability to pull you out of Red Zone if you are in it or getting into it. For example, with the practice of self-awareness in the Blue Zone, you can get out of the Red Zone much more quickly and easily than other times. If you have a strong sense of love, appreciation, empathy and compassion, you may rarely, if ever, experience Red Zone emotions. However, the goal is not to never feel a negative emotion. Rather, it is to have a sense of power, control and mastery over your emotions so you are not controlled by them and your life is not dominated by them. If you are able to be in Green or Blue Zone, you have a lot more power and strength over what you want to experience and feel, rather than what you may feel you are a victim of. The Green Zone and Blue Zone take an individual out of victim patterns, and into a space of more strength, giving, and a greater, more expansive life. Similar to the Green Zone, the Blue Zone has blended positive emotions, and is not necessarily a bottom-up experience. However, the Blue Zone is arguably a higher level of positive emotion than the Green and Red Zones.

BLUE ZONE: UPLIFTING & LIGHTENING EMOTIONS

Bliss, Serenity, Peace, Harmony, Self-Awareness, Balance
Joy, Enthusiasm, Abundance, Exhilaration, Hope

Compassion, Empathy, Inspiration, Clarity, Presence
Love, Appreciation, Gratitude, Devotion, Generosity

Foundational Components of Happiness-Based Mindfulness:
The Freedom 'Purple' Zone

The Purple Zone is another component of the Happiness-Based Mindfulness, Emotion Chart. The Purple Zone is categorized as focused on freedom emotions and the stabilization or maintenance of positive emotions. This is demonstrated by the symbol of a triangle, where the third element is the 'stabilizer.' This is in juxtaposition to the other emotion zones of blue, green and red that are categorized by more of a 'seesaw' up and down movement. When one (perceived) negative experience, thought or emotion happens, it moves the experiencer in a Red Zone downward trajectory. When a (perceived) positive experience, thought or emotion happens, it moves the experiencer in an upward direction out of the Red Zone and into the Green or Blue Zones. However, this can create an 'up and down' experience between the Red, Green and Blue Zones and is not inherently stable. This pushing away or pain from the (perceived) negative, and the grasping or holding on to the (perceived) positive, creates the up and down experience of the positive and negative, and that in itself is painful. Even when someone is in the Blue Zone (for example) they can have thoughts, feelings or experiences that push them back down. Being able to maintain the stability of the positive emotions, or a detachment to the negative is a powerful component of stabilization. The third element in the Purple Zone is a stabilizing element that helps to avoid the up and down experience. For example, if someone is able to be in a flow state, or have a general sense of mission/purpose or meaning in their life then they can maintain their wellbeing in spite of ups or downs in their life experiences. Also, other elements such as connection or a dedication to truth or goals, are also protective for the up and down experience that can occur. Other elements such as vision, faith, imagination, service, and creativity (for example) all exist within the Purple Zone. These elements are all important aspects in the Purple Zone for helping individuals to rise above their triggers that can cause the seesaw experience of emotions between the Red, Green, and Blue Zone. By focusing on something bigger, it helps to stabilize and free someone from the up and down triggers.

PURPLE ZONE: FREEDOM EMOTIONS

Unity, Big Picture Perspective, Integration, Freedom From 'Self', Seeing 'Self' in 'Other'

Compassion-Based Giving, Balance between 'Self' and 'Other,' Authenticity, Service, Creativity, Imagination, Faith, Inter-Dependence, Vision, Empowerment

Purpose, Meaning, Mission, Flow State, Connection, Truth, Beauty, Goals, Wisdom

Purple Zone Triangle

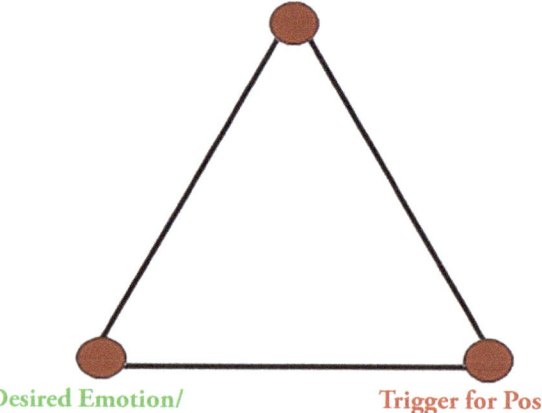

Purple Zone Stabilizer (Outside Focus Element)

Desired Emotion/
Experience

Trigger for Positive/
Negative Reaction

Red, Green, and Blue Zone 'Seesaw' of Positive and Negative Cycle

Desired Emotion/Experience   Trigger for Positive/Negative

Foundational Components of Happiness-Based Mindfulness: *Transcendence 'Yellow' Zone*

The Yellow Zone refers to the area of Transcendence, or going beyond certain issues. If an individual is in the space of the Yellow Zone it means they are assessing for issues or concerns you've gone beyond. It helps for seeing what you no longer are concerned with and what issues on some level you have 'graduated from.' The Yellow Zone is beyond the Purple Zone, because the experiencer is no longer concerned with stabilizing or maintaining an experience, they have in fact gone beyond the experience and it's something they may feel is in their past.

Transcendence

The Emotion Chart in Summary

The Emotion Chart and the various color zones all work together in various ways to understand how to navigate, manage, and improve one's emotional state. It is also an effective tool for individuals to use independently to check in and manage their emotions, and as an everyday management tool for improving and maintaining positive mental health and wellness. It is significant to understand each color zone and how it impacts well-being, as well as how all the aspects of the chart work together for happiness.

Foundational Components of Happiness-Based Mindfulness: Trapped Cycles Diagram

The trapped cycles diagram is a tool to help you identify where or how you may feel stuck or trapped in your life. A major barrier to happiness is having feelings of being trapped, stuck, or powerless to influence the direction you want to go. However, one of the first steps to identifying if there is a cycle you are stuck in is to look and notice. This diagram helps to identify any particular thoughts, beliefs, reactions, or emotional states you may be stuck in and repeating. The first step to breaking and getting out of cycles and repeating patterns is to see, non-judgmentally, what the patterns are. By observing the pattern, in a detachment way, and noticing what is happening…you begin to disempower the cycle that you may feel stuck in. When you observe, you are not reacting and participating, you are detached and an observer.

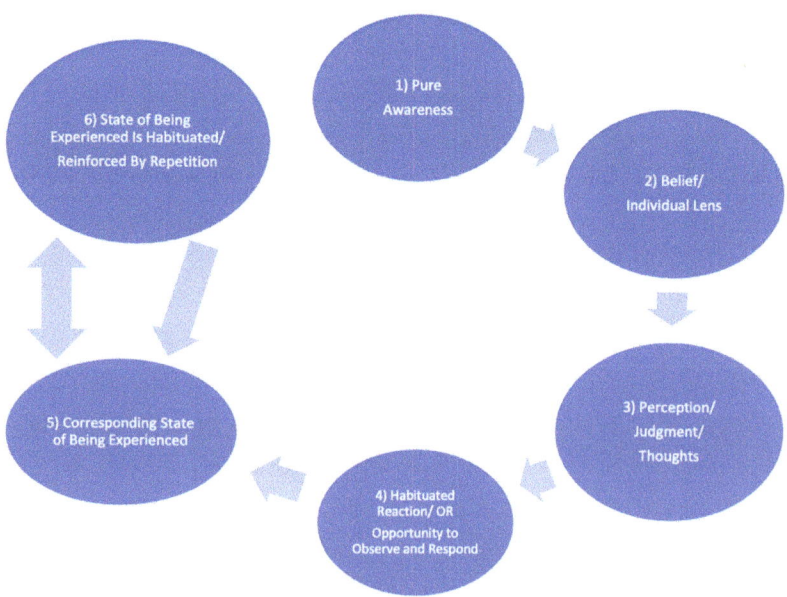

Foundational Components of Happiness-Based Mindfulness: Compassion-Based Mindfulness Chart

Another important tool in this Compassion-Based Happiness Workshop is the Compassion-Based Mindfulness Chart. This chart is provided below and helps you to identify your level of compassion towards yourself and others. Compassion towards oneself and others is a critical part of happiness and improving happiness. It also helps with managing stress, emotional regulation, and breaking out of harmful cycles. Through a daily reflection on self-compassion and compassion towards others, we can easily improve our well-being and self-esteem, and free ourselves from destructive patterns.

Compassion-Based Resiliency Chart

Full, Unconditional Compassion to Self and Others
Full Compassion to Self and Others
Partial Compassion to Self and Others
Neutral on Compassion to Self and Others
Partial Negative Judgement of Self and Others
Full Negative Judgement of Self and Others
Don't Understand or Know What This Means
Unconscious Reactions, Habits and Patterns

Foundational Components of Happiness-Based Mindfulness: Inquiry Questions...

A key component of the Happiness-Based Mindfulness Approach is reflection and self-awareness. Self-inquiry questions are an important component of this. For example, regarding the Emotion Chart, it may be helpful to ask yourself about the parts of the chart you experience most often, and what parts you would like to experience. For the compassion chart, it may be helpful to ask yourself how compassionate you are to yourself, and towards others. For the Trapped Cycle Diagram, it can be helpful to ask about cycles you may feel stuck in in your life, or any cycles you feel you've freed yourself from. The practice of inquiry is a practice of self-reflection and self-awareness. It is very powerful for change and to get out of negative patterns you may be stuck in. The charts and diagrams from the Happiness-Based Mindfulness program are meant to be tools for deeper self-awareness and self-inquiry.

Tools and Applications of Happiness-Based Mindfulness (HBM)

Journey Through the HBM

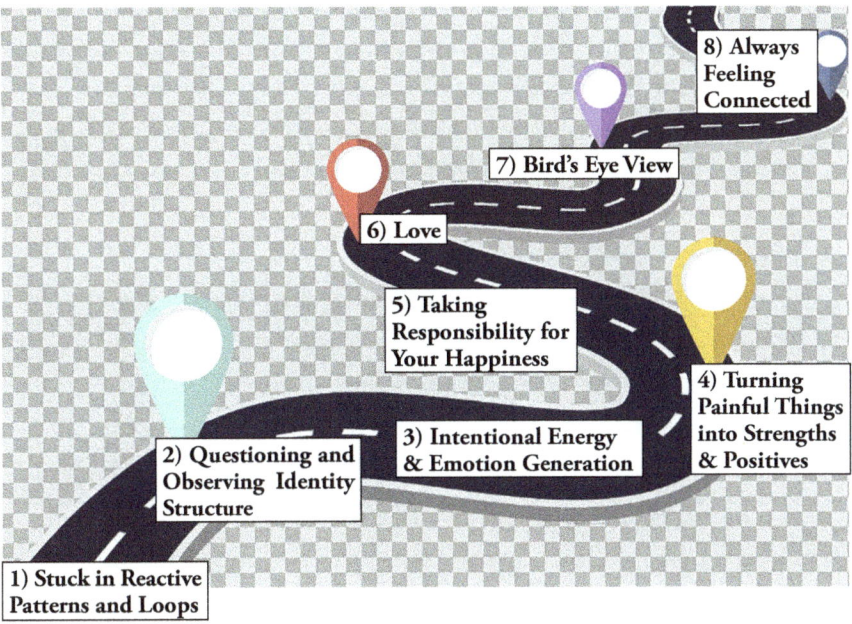

Overview of the HBM

Happiness-Based Mindfulness is designed to help improve the lived experience of happiness in your everyday life. The most extensive form contains twelve modules and incorporates key components of happiness and well-being in every module. These modules include practical tools that can be implemented in everyday life. In this program, the term 'happiness' means a state of contentment and satisfaction regardless of one's situation. Happiness may be experienced as a temporary state, but aspects that comprise happiness like a sense of purpose, connection, meaning, and working towards a higher purpose are more stable and long-lasting.

The modules include recurring key components. These contain 1) understanding your identity structure and assessing what you want it to be instead of accepting already prescribed programs; 2) understanding any loops or patterns you may feel trapped in and how to get out; 3) an understanding of how we are generators of emotion and how to take our power back and the energy we want to generate; 4) bringing awareness to our levels of happiness regularly as a method to increase well-being; 5) accountability and responsibility for your lived experience of happiness and what you would like to change or accept; 6) bringing more love and kindness into your life as a method to increase your happiness; and 7) connection as a means of sustainable happiness. These concepts are implemented in practical, easy-to-understand ways throughout the course with weekly meetings, hypnotherapy meditations, and daily exercises.

Compassion–Based Happiness 1-Hour Workshop

Created by
Sara Spowart, PhD, DMFT, LMFT, MPA, MA

Table of Contents

This 1-2 hour workshop is titled "Compassion-Based Happiness" and incorporates key concepts of the Happiness-Based Mindfulness program. In this workshop, these components include the Emotion Chart, The Trapped Cycles Diagram, The Compassion-Based Mindfulness Chart, inquiry questions, and discussion opportunities. Below are the guiding principles for the workshop.

1. Overview...

This one-hour workshop includes the Emotion Chart, the Trapped Cycles Diagram, the Compassion-Based Mindfulness Chart, A Compassion-Based Meditation and inquiry questions. The Emotion Chart is a mindfulness tool to help you identify which emotions you tend to experience, and what you'd like to experience. It also helps provide greater insight, detachment and understanding for emotional challenges you may regularly experience. The Trapped Cycles Diagram is a tool to help you identify, with detachment and awareness, any cycles you may be caught in either with thoughts, behaviors, patterns or emotions. The first step to freeing yourself from a trapped cycle is fostering an awareness and detachment of the cycle you have been in. The Compassion-Based Mindfulness Chart is an opportunity to increase happiness through awareness and identification of areas in your life you can improve compassion, and an understanding of how compassionate you are to yourself and others. The Compassion-Based meditation is meant to foster and support greater relaxation and compassion building for yourself and others. Lastly, the inquiry questions throughout are designed to improve happiness, self-awareness and insight.

2. **The first activity is the Emotion Chart. Please reflect on or discuss a time you felt you were strongly stuck in a certain area of the chart such as the "red, green, blue, purple zones" (10-15 minutes)**

PURPLE ZONE: FREEDOM EMOTIONS

Unity, Big Picture Perspective, Integration, Freedom From 'Self', Seeing 'Self' in 'Other'

Compassion-Based Giving, Balance between 'Self' and 'Other,' Authenticity, Service, Creativity, Imagination, Faith, Inter-Dependence, Vision, Empowerment

Purpose, Meaning, Mission, Flow State, Connection, Truth, Beauty, Goals, Wisdom

BLUE ZONE: UPLIFTING & LIGHTENING EMOTIONS

Bliss, Serenity, Peace, Harmony, Self-Awareness, Balance Joy, Enthusiasm, Abundance, Exhilaration, Hope

Compassion, Empathy, Inspiration, Clarity, Presence Love, Appreciation, Gratitude, Devotion, Generosity

GREEN ZONE: RELIEF EMOTIONS

Cooperation, Trust, Letting Go, Detachment Satisfaction, Amusement, Curiosity

Power, Strength, Agency, Discovery, Challenge, Discipline Self-Esteem, Dignity, Duty, Obligation Neutral, Acceptance, Contentment, Safety Happy, Excited, Surprised, Fun

RED ZONE: DESTRUCTIVE & CYCLICAL EMOTIONS

Anxiety, Nervousness, Shock, Confusion, Control, Stressed, Co-Dependent Anger, Rage, Avoidance Guilt, Resentment Fear, Hatred, Blame, Denial, Self-Centeredness Sadness, Grief, Loss

Isolated, Disconnected, Lonely, Duality Hopelessness, Resignation, Depression Powerlessness, Overwhelm, Frozen, Terror, Trauma Shame, Apathy, Helplessness

Inquiry...

a. *What part of the chart do you think you are most often?*

b. *What part of the chart would you like to be in more often?*

3. **The Trapped Cycles Diagram and discussing about one time you, or someone you knew, was trapped in a repeating cycle and how they knew or experienced being trapped (10-15 minutes)**

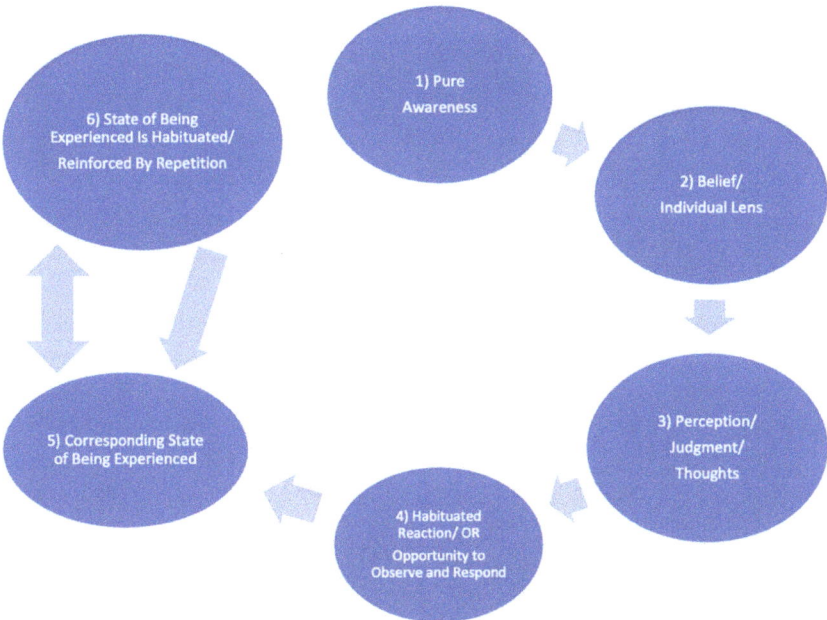

Inquiry...

a. *What is a cycle you have felt stuck in in your life?*

b. *What is a cycle you freed yourself from in your life?*

4. **The Compassion-Based Mindfulness Chart and reflecting on how individual levels of compassion and mindfulness (10-15 minutes)**

Inquiry…

a. *Please discuss a time you were not particularly compassionate to yourself, and how did you know you weren't being compassionate to yourself?*

Compassion-Based Resiliency Chart

Full, Unconditional Compassion to Self and Others
Full Compassion to Self and Others
Partial Compassion to Self and Others
Neutral on Compassion to Self and Others
Partial Negative Judgement of Self and Others
Full Negative Judgement of Self and Others
Don't Understand or Know What This Means
Unconscious Reactions, Habits and Patterns

5. **Deep breathing exercise on breathing in compassion and breathing out self-kindness and with a compassionate inquiry to reflect on, and wrap up on key takeaways from the workshop (10-15 Minutes)**

Compassion, Self-Kindness, Safety & Rest Exercise:

Close your eyes and sit in a comfortable position, and maybe with your feet on the floor
Take a deep breath in through your nose and out through your mouth
Take another deep breath in through your nose and out through your mouth
Take one more deep breath in through your nose and out through your mouth

And as I count down from 5 to 1, feeling more and more relaxed, calm and at peace
5 to 4 feeling more relaxed
4 to 3
3 to 2 calmer and calmer
2 to 1 feeling calm, relaxed and at peace

Imagine that you are sitting near a grassy green field and peaceful forest
Breath in peace and calm
Breath out the feeling of support and safety
Notice the breath in and out and the flow of the air

Now, imagine you are standing up and then are walking towards the forest
As you walk towards the forest, you feel more and more supported, calm and at peace
Deep breath in and out, allowing yourself in this moment to be safe and supported
Breathing in support and compassion
Breathing out support and compassion

Then imagine that you are wearing a back-pack full of rocks, and these rocks are everything and anything that is weighing you down, causing you trauma, stress, pain and fear

You walk over to a lake in the forest, and this lake dissolves any and all the rocks in your backpack
One by one throwing these rocks into the lake, and they melt and dissolve away
3
2
And 1
These rocks melt and dissolve away completely
And throwing your backpack into the lake now, and it dissolves away completely
And you feel lighter and lighter, more and more at peace and at ease
Deep breath in and out,
Imagining yourself sitting in this forest by the lake
And you are filled with rest

Your head, neck and shoulders...in this moment, you feel kindness and compassion foryourself
Your arms and hands ....in this moment, your arms and hands are filled with compassion and self-kindness
Your torso, heart, chest, and stomach...kindness and compassion
Your back, hips, legs and feet...all filled with kindness and compassion

And you breathe in a feeling of compassion, and breath out
Knowing that in this moment, you are filled with compassion, love and feel at peace...

Inquiry Questions (approximately 10-15 minutes)

After completing these exercises, what did you notice? A key component of this workshop is reflection and self-awareness. Self-inquiry questions are an important aspect of this. For example, regarding the Emotion Chart, it may be helpful to ask yourself about the parts of the chart you experience most often, and what parts you would like to experience. For the compassion chart, it may be helpful to ask yourself how compassionate you are to yourself, and towards others.

For the Trapped Cycle Diagram, it can be helpful to ask about cycles you may feel stuck in in your life, or any cycles you feel you've freed yourself from. The practice of inquiry is a practice of self-reflection and self-awareness. It is very powerful for change and to get out of negative patterns you may be stuck in. The charts and diagrams from this workshop are meant to be tools for deeper self-awareness and self-inquiry.

Inquiry Questions to Consider...

a. *What did you notice from the activities?*

b. *What is one key takeaway from this workshop today?*

c. *If you can summarize how you feel right now in one word, what would that one word be?*

Brief Trauma-Focused HBM

Created by
Sara Spowart, PhD, DMFT, LMFT, MPA, MA

Table of Contents

Session 1: Helpless and Powerless

When major life changes, stressors, or traumas occur, we can feel lost, confused, helpless, and powerless. Everything we thought we knew could be destroyed or in chaos. It can seem impossible to know what to trust or count on, or how to make sense of the tragedies, extreme stress, and suffering.

In this session, we work on and explore understanding the Emotion Chart Exercise and the Red, Green, Blue and Purple zones of this chart. We also explore discussion and reflection on the emotions we are currently experiencing and how to go from feelings of helplessness and powerlessness into greater strength, resilience, and hope. This exercise is also continued in Session 2.

In addition to this, we work on the topic of compassion in this session through the Compassion-Based Resiliency Exercise. Compassion here refers to a sense of kindness and love, combined with insight and understanding of life situations. This compassion refers not only to compassion for ourselves but also for others and our life situations. Our levels of compassion help impact our resiliency, recovery, mindset, and perspective. They can bring ease to challenging circumstances and uplift us in times of crisis.

Lastly in session 1, there is the Nervous System, Safety, and Rest Exercise. This is a relaxation, deep breathing, meditation exercise meant to help reduce nervous system distress. In times of crisis, extreme stress, and trauma, exercises that help calm the nervous system can be deeply beneficial and help to reset our systems. If our nerves are on overdrive from traumatic stress, it greatly heightens the chances of physical and mental illness. It also makes it much more challenging to manage everyday stressors and life functioning. This exercise is continued also in Session 2.

First Exercise:

1. ***The Emotion Chart Exercise*** *(approximately 15 minutes):*

PURPLE ZONE: FREEDOM EMOTIONS

Unity, Big Picture Perspective, Integration, Freedom From 'Self', Seeing 'Self' in 'Other'

Compassion-Based Giving, Balance between 'Self' and 'Other,' Authenticity, Service, Creativity, Imagination, Faith, Inter-Dependence, Vision, Empowerment

Purpose, Meaning, Mission, Flow State, Connection, Truth, Beauty, Goals, Wisdom

BLUE ZONE: UPLIFTING & LIGHTENING EMOTIONS

Bliss, Serenity, Peace, Harmony, Self-Awareness, Balance
Joy, Enthusiasm, Abundance, Exhilaration, Hope

Compassion, Empathy, Inspiration, Clarity, Presence
Love, Appreciation, Gratitude, Devotion, Generosity

GREEN ZONE: RELIEF EMOTIONS

Cooperation, Trust, Letting Go, Detachment
Satisfaction, Amusement, Curiosity

Power, Strength, Agency, Discovery, Challenge, Discipline
Self-Esteem, Dignity, Duty, Obligation
Neutral, Acceptance, Contentment, Safety
Happy, Excited, Surprised, Fun

RED ZONE: DESTRUCTIVE & CYCLICAL EMOTIONS

Anxiety, Nervousness, Shock, Confusion, Control, Stressed, Co-Dependent
Anger, Rage, Avoidance
Guilt, Resentment
Fear, Hatred, Blame, Denial, Self-Centeredness
Sadness, Grief, Loss

Isolated, Disconnected, Lonely, Duality
Hopelessness, Resignation, Depression
Powerlessness, Overwhelm, Frozen, Terror, Trauma
Shame, Apathy, Helplessness

Reflection and Discussion Questions:

a. Where have you been in the chart today or right now...the *Red, Green,* and/or *Blue Zones*?

b. How much are you in these different zones?

c. What emotions do you most frequently experience?

Second Exercise:

2. *The Compassion-Based Resiliency Exercise*
(approximately 30-45 minutes):

Reflection and Discussion Questions:

a. What does *compassion* mean for you?

b. What does *compassion for others* mean?

c. When are some moments you have experienced some level of compassion? What did it feel like?

d. What is an area of your life in which you can apply greater levels of compassion to yourself or others currently? How can you apply this compassion?

e. What is something that has happened in the past where you can apply greater levels of compassion for yourself or others? How can you apply this compassion?

f. Please refer to the Compassion-Based Resiliency chart below. Where in the chart do you feel you have been recently?

Compassion-Based Resiliency Chart

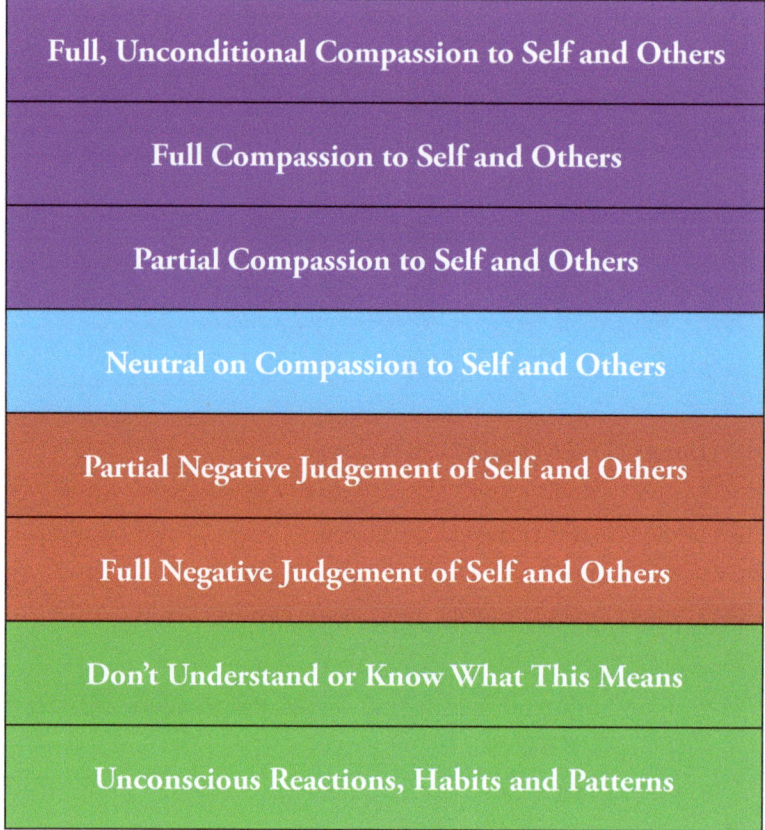

Full, Unconditional Compassion to Self and Others

Full Compassion to Self and Others

Partial Compassion to Self and Others

Neutral on Compassion to Self and Others

Partial Negative Judgement of Self and Others

Full Negative Judgement of Self and Others

Don't Understand or Know What This Means

Unconscious Reactions, Habits and Patterns

Third Exercise:

3. *The Nervous System, Safety & Rest Exercise*
(approximately 15 minutes):

Close your eyes and sit in a comfortable position, and maybe with your feet on the floor
Take a deep breath in through your nose and out through your mouth
Take another deep breath in through your nose and out through your mouth
Take one more deep breath in through your nose and out through your mouth

And as I count down from 5 to 1, feeling more and more relaxed, calm and at peace
5 to 4 feeling more relaxed
4 to 3
3 to 2 calmer and calmer
2 to 1 feeling calm, relaxed and at peace

Imagine that you are sitting near a grassy green field and peaceful forest
Breath in peace and calm
Breath out the feeling of support and safety
Notice the breath in and out and the flow of the air

Now, imagine you are standing up and then are walking towards the forest
As you walk towards the forest, you feel more and more supported, calm and at peace
Deep breath in and out, allowing yourself in this moment to be safe and supported
Breathing in support and compassion
Breathing out support and compassion

Then imagine that you are wearing a back-pack full of rocks, and these rocks are everything and anything that is weighing you down, causing you trauma, stress, pain and fear
You walk over to a lake in the forest, and this lake dissolves any and all the rocks in your backpack

One by one throwing these rocks into the lake, and they melt and dissolve away

3

2

And 1

These rocks melt and dissolve away completely

And throwing your backpack into the lake now, and it dissolves away completely

And you feel lighter and lighter, more and more at peace and at ease

Deep breath in and out,

Imagining yourself sitting in this forest by the lake

And you are filled with rest

Your head, neck and shoulders…in this moment, you feel kindness and compassion for yourself

Your arms and hands ….in this moment, your arms and hands are filled with compassion and self-kindness

Your torso, heart, chest, and stomach…kindness and compassion

Your back, hips, legs and feet…all filled with kindness and compassion

And you breathe in a feeling of compassion, and breath out

Knowing that in this moment, you are filled with compassion, love and feel at peace…

Session 2: Positive, Resilient Self

When an individual or group experiences trauma, severe stress, violence, powerlessness, hopelessness, or other things similar to this… it is not unusual to struggle with self-worth and self-confidence. Survivors of trauma or abuse often suffer from lower self-esteem, and negative, depressive thought patterns, and blame themselves for what they have experienced. This can be a way to cope with and try to make sense of things that are beyond our understanding. However, ultimately, negativity towards the self, negative thought patterns or beliefs, and staying in the victim or weakened mindset, only makes things worse in the end.

Our ability to foster and support a positive, resilient self is essential for strengthening ourselves to handle difficult, or traumatic life circumstances. No matter what the situation is, we can shift our mindset or perspective to help us become stronger and more empowered. The exercises covered in this session include the Emotion Chart Exercise, The Positive Identity Layers Exercise, and The Nervous System, Safety & Rest Exercise.

The Emotion Chart Exercise is meant to help foster an awareness and comprehension of what emotions you are experiencing and the main zones you are living in whether these are the red, green, blue, purple zones or some combination.

The Positive Identity Layers Exercise is meant to help identify and reflect on what beliefs or thoughts you hold about yourself, your community, and your situation. It is an opportunity to reflect on how you view yourself, your community, and your environment and any beliefs you'd like to keep or change to better empower yourself. A positive identity is very powerful for resiliency and optimism in your strengths and abilities, and the ability to manage traumatic and high-stress situations. The way we view ourselves, others, and our community is powerful for how we navigate unknown or traumatic life circumstances and get beyond them.

The Nervous System, Safety & Rest Exercise is the last exercise in this session and is also significant in its ability to foster and support greater inner strength, resiliency, and healing. Trauma and severe stress due to humanitarian situations and disasters can be very hard on the nervous system and our daily lives. It can negatively impact our thinking, mindset, and ability to rebuild or navigate challenging circumstances, thrive, be successful, and heal. By calming the nervous system, we can experience greater restoration, healing, and even post-traumatic growth after severely stressful and painful life situations. It is recommended to do this exercise or a similar one every day to help calm the mind, body, and nervous system, no matter what the circumstances may be.

First Exercise:

1. *Emotion Chart Exercise* (*approximately 15 minutes*):

PURPLE ZONE: FREEDOM EMOTIONS

Unity, Big Picture Perspective, Integration, Freedom From 'Self', Seeing 'Self' in 'Other'

Compassion-Based Giving, Balance between 'Self' and 'Other,' Authenticity, Service, Creativity, Imagination, Faith, Inter-Dependence, Vision, Empowerment

Purpose, Meaning, Mission, Flow State, Connection, Truth, Beauty, Goals, Wisdom

BLUE ZONE: UPLIFTING & LIGHTENING EMOTIONS

Bliss, Serenity, Peace, Harmony, Self-Awareness, Balance Joy, Enthusiasm, Abundance, Exhilaration, Hope

Compassion, Empathy, Inspiration, Clarity, Presence Love, Appreciation, Gratitude, Devotion, Generosity

GREEN ZONE: RELIEF EMOTIONS

Cooperation, Trust, Letting Go, Detachment Satisfaction, Amusement, Curiosity

Power, Strength, Agency, Discovery, Challenge, Discipline Self-Esteem, Dignity, Duty, Obligation Neutral, Acceptance, Contentment, Safety Happy, Excited, Surprised, Fun

RED ZONE: DESTRUCTIVE & CYCLICAL EMOTIONS

Anxiety, Nervousness, Shock, Confusion, Control, Stressed, Co-Dependent Anger, Rage, Avoidance Guilt, Resentment Fear, Hatred, Blame, Denial, Self-Centeredness Sadness, Grief, Loss

Isolated, Disconnected, Lonely, Duality Hopelessness, Resignation, Depression Powerlessness, Overwhelm, Frozen, Terror, Trauma Shame, Apathy, Helplessness

Reflection and Discussion Questions:

a. Where have you been in the chart today or right now…the *Red, Green, Blue, and/or Purple Zones*?

b. How much are you in these different zones?

c. What is a "Blue or Green Zone" emotion you'd like to experience more of? How can you do 5 minutes a day of something small to bring this experience into your life?

Second Exercise:

2. ***The Positive Identity Layers Exercise*** *(approximately 20 minutes):*

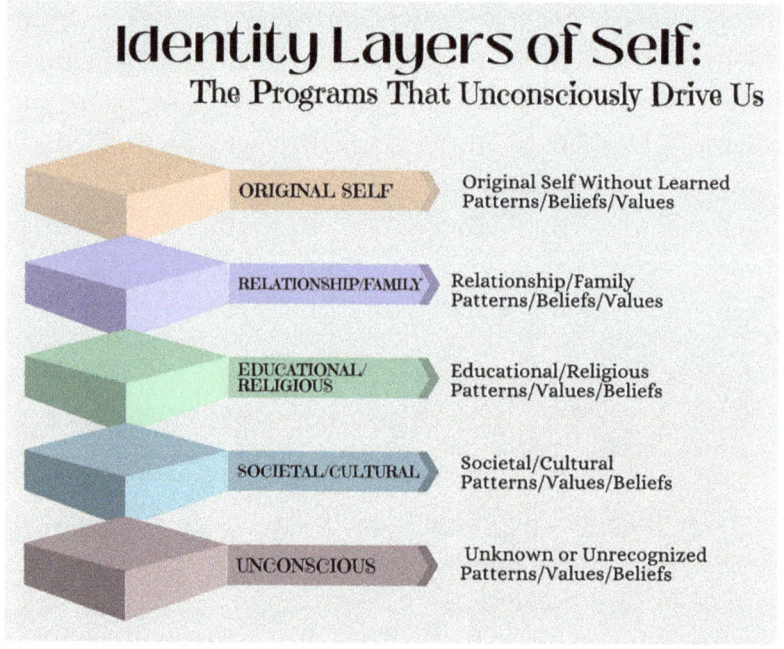

Reflection and Discussion Questions:

a. What are some patterns, values, or beliefs you hold about yourself that are positive?

b. What are some patterns, values, or beliefs you hold about your family and close friends that are positive?

c. What are some patterns, values, or beliefs you hold about your community that are positive?

d. Are there any patterns, values, or beliefs you would like to have and add to your life that are positive?

Third Exercise:

3. *The Nervous System, Safety & Rest Exercise*
    (approximately 15 minutes):

Close your eyes and sit in a comfortable position, and maybe with your feet on the floor
Take a deep breath in through your nose and out through your mouth
Take another deep breath in through your nose and out through your mouth
Take one more deep breath in through your nose and out through your mouth

And as I count down from 5 to 1, feeling more and more relaxed, calm and at peace
5 to 4 feeling more relaxed
4 to 3
3 to 2 calmer and calmer
2 to 1 feeling calm, relaxed and at peace

Imagine that you are sitting near a grassy green field and peaceful forest
Breath in peace and calm

Breath out the feeling of support and safety
Notice the breath in and out and the flow of the air

Now, imagine you are standing up and then are walking towards the forest
As you walk towards the forest, you feel more and more supported, calm and at peace
Deep breath in and out, allowing yourself in this moment to be safe and supported
Breathing in support and compassion
Breathing out support and compassion

Then imagine that you are wearing a back-pack full of rocks, and these rocks are everything and anything that is weighing you down, causing you trauma, stress, pain and fear
You walk over to a lake in the forest, and this lake dissolves any and all the rocks in your backpack
One by one throwing these rocks into the lake, and they melt and dissolve away
3
2
And 1
These rocks melt and dissolve away completely
And throwing your backpack into the lake now, and it dissolves away completely
And you feel lighter and lighter, more and more at peace and at ease
Deep breath in and out,
Imagining yourself sitting in this forest by the lake
And you are filled with rest

Your head, neck and shoulders…in this moment, you feel kindness and compassion foryourself
Your arms and hands ….in this moment, your arms and hands are filled with compassion and self-kindness
Your torso, heart, chest, and stomach…kindness and compassion
Your back, hips, legs and feet…all filled with kindness and compassion

And you breathe in a feeling of compassion, and breath out
Knowing that in this moment, you are filled with compassion, love and feel at peace…

Session 3: Feeling Better

In this session, we look at our innate ability and the application of certain practices that can help bring greater freedom from suffering. There is a balance between validating and honoring our experiences, and being free from their pain of them so we can thrive and somehow improve our situations. Part of overcoming suffering from traumatic life events or chronic toxic stress is to honor and validate what you have experienced and have compassion for yourself and your suffering. Even if what you experienced is considered 'normal' in your community, family, or society, it doesn't mean it didn't have a negative, painful impact. It doesn't mean things weren't done that were wrong or extremely harmful. However, normalizing or ignoring that pain and the experiences unfortunately will not make it go away. It can create harmful coping mechanisms or patterns that do not help you thrive and overcome and create issues like panic, severe anxiety, trauma symptoms, depression, hopelessness, and even suicidal ideation. However, if we become extremely focused on our pain and suffering and what we have experienced, and it even becomes part of our identity that is also problematic. There is a balance and middle way to manage extreme suffering or trauma so it does not consume or define you or your life in the long term. The things that have happened in your life, the experiences you've had, and your current life situation doesn't have to be the end of your story or your identity. We can find a way to turn it into motivation for change, rebuilding, and growth.

In this session, we work on three exercises. The first is the Honor Your Suffering Exercise. In this, we work to validate and honor what we, others, or our community have experienced that has created trauma and great pain. The goal is not to become stuck in the pain, but rather to honor and acknowledge it for the power it has and our own unique experience of it. Then to apply compassion to the pain and ourselves. The second exercise in this session is the Adapted Rational

Emotive Behavior Therapy (REBT) Exercise. This is an opportunity to learn a tangible skill to help transform negative thoughts, feelings, or beliefs into alternative, positive ones. The goal of this exercise is to provide information on a tangible skill that can be applied daily independently even after the session is done. The more you practice this activity, the more it becomes part of your everyday mindset and will help you manage stress, negative emotions, and future events. The third exercise is the Blue Zone Emotion Chart Exercise. This is adapted from the Emotion Chart Exercise conducted in the first and second sessions. The goal of this activity is to cultivate a greater focus on positive, 'blue zone' emotions and bring greater awareness to these emotions. By practicing noticing when you are having those emotions, and intentionally trying to create moments where you feel blue-zone emotions, you create more neuropathways in the brain that allow for more blue-zone thoughts and feelings. You also start to intentionally create more goodness in your life, even if it's just a small shift every day, or 1% happier every day or every week. Over time this adds up when we intentionally try to focus on experiencing a few moments in the Blue Zone.

First Exercise:

1. ***Honor Your Pain Exercise*** *(approximately 20 minutes):*

a. Please list at least 5 things that are upsetting you or 5 emotions you are struggling with such as guilt, anxiety, helplessness, powerlessness, overwhelm, sadness, fear, depression, stress, or shame.

b. Please discuss or write for 10 minutes on at least one of these 5 things

c. Then please reflect on compassion for these five things

Second Exercise:

2. ***Adapted Rational Emotive Behavior Therapy (REBT) Exercise*** *(approximately 20 minutes):*

a. Please reflect on a negative thought or belief you have
b. Please discuss or write how this negative thought or belief may benefit you (usually it is a protective reason)
c. Please discuss or write how this negative thought or belief may harm you (usually it worsens life situation or negative emotions and puts you more in the 'Red Zone')
d. Please discuss or write at least 3 positive alternatives to this negative thought or belief

1 Negative Identified Belief:

What is the benefit of this negatively identified belief?

What is the harm of this negatively identified belief?

3 Positive Alternatives to Identified Belief:

a.

b.

c.

Third Exercise:

3. *Blue Zone Emotion Chart Exercise* *(approximately 10 minutes):*

a. Please look at the Blue Zone area of the chart below.

b. Are there any moments you experienced in the blue zone, even if it was 1 minute or less recently?

c. What blue zone emotion did you experience and why?

d. Can you try to create more Blue Zone emotions every day? If yes, which emotion would you like to try to focus on?

Uplifting and Lighening Emotions
Bliss, Serenity, Peace, Harmony, Self-Awareness, Balance
Joy, Enthusiasm, Abundance, Exhilaration, Hope
Compassion, Empathy, Inspiration, Clarity, Presence
Love, Appreciation, Gratitude, Devotion, Generosity

Resources for the Sessions:

A. Emotion Chart

PURPLE ZONE: FREEDOM EMOTIONS

*Unity, Big Picture Perspective, Integration, Freedom From 'Self',
Seeing 'Self' in 'Other'*

*Compassion-Based Giving, Balance between 'Self' and 'Other,'
Authenticity, Service, Creativity, Imagination, Faith, Inter-
Dependence, Vision, Empowerment*

*Purpose, Meaning, Mission, Flow State, Connection, Truth, Beauty,
Goals, Wisdom*

BLUE ZONE: UPLIFTING & LIGHTENING EMOTIONS

*Bliss, Serenity, Peace, Harmony, Self-Awareness, Balance
Joy, Enthusiasm, Abundance, Exhilaration, Hope*

*Compassion, Empathy, Inspiration, Clarity, Presence
Love, Appreciation, Gratitude, Devotion, Generosity*

GREEN ZONE: RELIEF EMOTIONS

*Cooperation, Trust, Letting Go, Detachment
Satisfaction, Amusement, Curiosity*

*Power, Strength, Agency, Discovery, Challenge, Discipline
Self-Esteem, Dignity, Duty, Obligation
Neutral, Acceptance, Contentment, Safety
Happy, Excited, Surprised, Fun*

RED ZONE: DESTRUCTIVE & CYCLICAL EMOTIONS

*Anxiety, Nervousness, Shock, Confusion, Control, Stressed, Co-Dependent
Anger, Rage, Avoidance
Guilt, Resentment
Fear, Hatred, Blame, Denial, Self-Centeredness
Sadness, Grief, Loss*

*Isolated, Disconnected, Lonely, Duality
Hopelessness, Resignation, Depression
Powerlessness, Overwhelm, Frozen, Terror, Trauma
Shame, Apathy, Helplessness*

B. Adapted Rational Emotive Behavior Therapy (REBT) Exercises:
-Adapted and simplified by the creator of HBM, Sara Spowart, PhD, LMFT

Reframing Negative Beliefs Example:

Negative Identified Belief: *There's no reason to be happy*

What is the benefit of this negatively identified belief?
I get more attention from my family and others when I feel sad

What is the harm of this negatively identified belief?
Feeling bad, not helping mood, or wanting to stay sober

3 Positive Alternatives to Identified Belief:

a. There is at least one reason to be happy

b. Eventually there could be a reason to be happy

c. I am mostly just hurting myself with this belief

C. Identity Layers Chart: Which layer are you most affected by?
-Made by HBM creator, Sara Spowart, PhD, LMFT

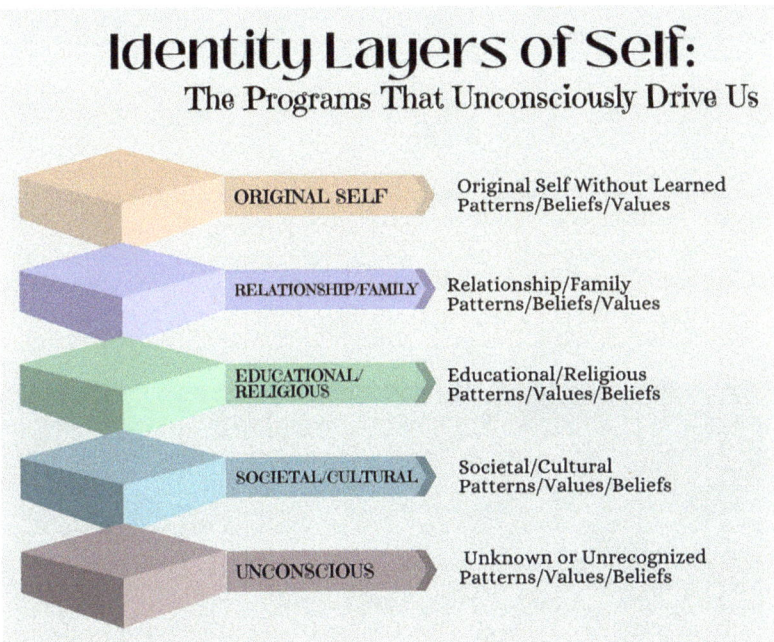

Identity Layers of Self:
The Programs That Unconsciously Drive Us

ORIGINAL SELF — Original Self Without Learned Patterns/Beliefs/Values

RELATIONSHIP/FAMILY — Relationship/Family Patterns/Beliefs/Values

EDUCATIONAL/RELIGIOUS — Educational/Religious Patterns/Values/Beliefs

SOCIETAL/CULTURAL — Societal/Cultural Patterns/Values/Beliefs

UNCONSCIOUS — Unknown or Unrecognized Patterns/Values/Beliefs

D. Adapted Rational Emotive Behavior Therapy (REBT) Exercise
-Made by HBM creator, Sara Spowart, PhD, LMFT

1 Negative Identified Belief:

a. What is the benefit of this negatively identified belief?

b. What is the harm of this negatively identified belief?

3 Positive Alternatives to Identified Belief:

a.

b.

c.

E. Compassion-Based Resiliency Chart
-Made by HBM creator, Sara Spowart, PhD, LMFT

Full, Unconditional Compassion to Self and Others
Full Compassion to Self and Others
Partial Compassion to Self and Others
Neutral on Compassion to Self and Others
Partial Negative Judgement of Self and Others
Full Negative Judgement of Self and Others
Don't Understand or Know What This Means
Unconscious Reactions, Habits and Patterns

F. The Nervous System, Safety & Rest Exercise

*Close your eyes and sit in a comfortable position, and maybe with your feet on
the floor*
Take a deep breath in through your nose and out through your mouth
Take another deep breath in through your nose and out through your mouth
Take one more deep breath in through your nose and out through your mouth

And as I count down from 5 to 1, feeling more and more relaxed, calm and at peace
5 to 4 feeling more relaxed
4 to 3
3 to 2 calmer and calmer
2 to 1 feeling calm, relaxed and at peace

Imagine that you are sitting near a grassy green field and peaceful forest
Breath in peace and calm
Breath out the feeling of support and safety
Notice the breath in and out and the flow of the air

Now, imagine you are standing up and then are walking towards the forest
As you walk towards the forest, you feel more and more supported, calm and at peace
Deep breath in and out, allowing yourself in this moment to be safe and supported
Breathing in support and compassion
Breathing out support and compassion

*Then imagine that you are wearing a back-pack full of rocks, and these rocks
are everything and anything that is weighing you down, causing you trauma,
stress, pain and fear*
*You walk over to a lake in the forest, and this lake dissolves any and all the rocks
in your backpack*
One by one throwing these rocks into the lake, and they melt and dissolve away
3
2
And 1
These rocks melt and dissolve away completely

And throwing your backpack into the lake now, and it dissolves away completely
And you feel lighter and lighter, more and more at peace and at ease
Deep breath in and out,
Imagining yourself sitting in this forest by the lake
And you are filled with rest

Your head, neck and shoulders…in this moment, you feel kindness and compassion for yourself
Your arms and hands ….in this moment, your arms and hands are filled with compassion and self-kindness
Your torso, heart, chest, and stomach…kindness and compassion
Your back, hips, legs and feet…all filled with kindness and compassion

And you breathe in a feeling of compassion, and breath out
Knowing that in this moment, you are filled with compassion, love and feel at peace…

For Instructors of Brief Trauma-Focused HBM:

1) Participate in all 3 sessions with a certified Brief Trauma-Focused HBM instructor and review the program, core concepts, course set-up, and activities.

2) Please complete the Brief Trauma-Focused HBM and all 3 sessions. Completing all activities and sessions will help you to be ready to teach so you are familiar with and have a deep understanding of the material.

3) Please read and reference all materials in the program and become familiar with the activities and their ongoing practice of them. This includes a comfortable use and regular application of all activities provided.

Happiness-Based Mindfulness
The 6-Week Happiness-Improvement Approach

Created by
Sara Spowart, PhD, DMFT, LMFT, MPA, MA

Table of Contents

Week 1: Trapped in Patterns and Loops

We have tens of thousands of thoughts a day, it's estimated that 90% of them are unconscious and about 90-95% are the same or very similar as the day before. This means that in many ways we are on autopilot, on repeat… and without awareness, we tend to stay on 'repeat' like a software program full of repeating codes.

Our automatic pilot patterns and stories can cause us pleasure or pain, and attachment to the stories (both positive and negative narratives) can also cause challenges. Being trapped in a cycle of the familiar, stuck in thought, belief, and feeling loops creates attachment and can keep us engaged in desired toxic lifestyles. However, the simple act of bringing awareness and identifying these patterns, loops, habits, and unconscious thought structures helps interrupt these loops.

Why does this matter? This matters because a majority of people spend most of their waking consciousness in an area I refer to as the "red zone" of emotions, meaning in a space of destructive emotions. Destructive emotions include such as shame, apathy, helplessness, blame, fear, resentment, anger, rage, guilt, sadness, depression, etc. They are emotions that hurt relationships, ourselves, and our societies. They are also emotions that tend to be re-enforcing. This means that fear tends to bring more fear and creates a mental pattern of living by fear. Anger tends to create more anger, and you can get trapped in a painful cycle of feeling angry, which creates more anger and challenges with managing or decreasing anger.

There are different ways of identifying patterns and modes of being. A skilled therapist can be very helpful, but instead of that, mindfulness, journaling through writing, or audio recordings can be helpful. Also, create a timeline of your experiences in your life and look for patterns. Another method is to look at the chart provided below and track the feelings regularly, multiple times a day to create and bring awareness to what you are experiencing. The simple identification of feelings, thoughts, habits, or patterns, is all that is needed in this step. You are allowing yourself to see more clearly. By noticing you are also becoming the 'observer' of something, instead of that thing itself, instead of the reaction itself. The more we can focus on the fact that we are not the emotions, habits, patterns, and feelings- we are a separate consciousness- the more we can see the trends we have been stuck in over time.

Resources for This Week:

A. Emotion Chart

PURPLE ZONE: FREEDOM EMOTIONS

Unity, Big Picture Perspective, Integration, Freedom From 'Self', Seeing 'Self' in 'Other'

Compassion-Based Giving, Balance between 'Self' and 'Other,' Authenticity, Service, Creativity, Imagination, Faith, Inter-Dependence, Vision, Empowerment

Purpose, Meaning, Mission, Flow State, Connection, Truth, Beauty, Goals, Wisdom

BLUE ZONE: UPLIFTING & LIGHTENING EMOTIONS

*Bliss, Serenity, Peace, Harmony, Self-Awareness, Balance
Joy, Enthusiasm, Abundance, Exhilaration, Hope*

*Compassion, Empathy, Inspiration, Clarity, Presence
Love, Appreciation, Gratitude, Devotion, Generosity*

GREEN ZONE: RELIEF EMOTIONS

*Cooperation, Trust, Letting Go, Detachment
Satisfaction, Amusement, Curiosity*

*Power, Strength, Agency, Discovery, Challenge, Discipline
Self-Esteem, Dignity, Duty, Obligation
Neutral, Acceptance, Contentment, Safety
Happy, Excited, Surprised, Fun*

RED ZONE: DESTRUCTIVE & CYCLICAL EMOTIONS

*Anxiety, Nervousness, Shock, Confusion, Control, Stressed, Co-Dependent
Anger, Rage, Avoidance
Guilt, Resentment
Fear, Hatred, Blame, Denial, Self-Centeredness
Sadness, Grief, Loss*

*Isolated, Disconnected, Lonely, Duality
Hopelessness, Resignation, Depression
Powerlessness, Overwhelm, Frozen, Terror, Trauma
Shame, Apathy, Helplessness*

B. Schedule of Zoom or Phone Meetings for 6-Week Course

Please be prepared to set aside approximately 1-2 hours a week over the 6 weeks for the successful completion of this course*

Week 1	1st Day of Program and Week 1 (30 Minute Meeting)
Week 2	2nd Meeting (30 Minute Meeting)
Week 3	3rd Meeting (30 Minute Meeting)
Week 4	4th Meeting (30 Minute Meeting)
Week 5	5th Meeting (30 Minute Meeting)
Week 6	6th Meeting (30 Minute Meeting)
Week 7	7th Meeting (30 Minute Meeting)

To Complete This Week:

1. *7 Days of Compassion-Based Insight:* To become free of patterns, habits, and the things that are blocking our happiness, first we must see and understand what is blocking and getting in the way. Awareness and mindfulness of what seems normal or habitual, are the first steps towards increasing happiness.

Please complete the reflections below for each day starting with day 1

2. *Self-Ratings:* **Please identify where you mostly are emotionally in the chart every day (red, green, blue and/or purple zones)**

3. *Meditations:* **Please listen to one of the available meditations at least twice this week.**

4. *Group/Individual Meetings:* **Please participate in the two meetings that occur in the first week.**

Day 1: Week 1

7 Days of Compassion-Based Insight: What is your narrative about yourself and your life? Have you seen yourself as a happy person, struggling person, stuck person, depressed, anxious, unloved, poor, rich, beautiful ugly, etc.? Please write or do an audio note on the above reflection questions

Self-Ratings: Identify where you mostly were emotionally in the chart today (red, green, blue, or purple zones).

Day 2: Week 1

7 Days of Compassion-Based Insight: How was your life this time last year? How were your thoughts, feelings, story, and perception of your life and your situation similar or different?
Please write or do an audio note for each question

Self-Ratings: Identify where you mostly were emotionally in the chart today (red, green, blue or purple zones).

Day 3: Week 1

7 Days of Compassion-Based Insight: How was your life this time 5 years ago? How were your thoughts, feelings, story, and perception of your life and your situation similar or different? Please write or do an audio note for each question

Self-Ratings: Identify where you mostly were emotionally in the chart today (red, green, blue, or purple zones).

Day 4: Week 1

7 Days of Compassion-Based Insight: How do you feel your life will be 1 year from now? How might your thoughts, feelings, story, and perception of your life and your situation be similar or different? Please write or do an audio note for each question

Self-Ratings: Identify where you mostly were emotionally in the chart today (red, green, or blue zone).

Day 5: Week 1

7 Days of Compassion-Based Insight: If there's anything you've ever felt trapped in, what would it be? What feels impossible to become free of? Please write or do an audio note for each question

Self-Ratings: Please identify where you mostly were emotionally in the chart today (red, green, blue or purple zones).

Day 6: Week 1

7 Days of Compassion-Based Insight: If you were in the 'blue zone' more often, what loops or patterns from the 'red zone' would be easier to manage when they get triggered?

Please write or do an audio note for each question

Self-Ratings: Please identify where you mostly were emotionally in the chart today (red, green, blue or purple zones).

Day 7: Week 1

7 Days of Compassion-Based Insight: What triggers get you accidentally into the red zone on the emotion chart? What helps you get into the blue zone? Please write or do an audio note for each question

Self-Ratings: Please identify where you mostly were emotionally in the chart today (red, green, blue or purple zones).

Please participate in either the 30-minute individual or group live compassion-based happiness program on Zoom on Day 7 to reflect, share, process, and have greater support.
Please feel free to send your writings/audio notes from this week to the instructor of the course.

Week 2: Your Identity Structure

Another aspect that is important for creating awareness and stopping attachment, engagement, and participation in harmful cycles is understanding your perception of yourself.

Some reflection questions to consider on this...

Who do you see yourself as? Who do others perceive you as?

What words would you use to describe yourself, both 'positive' and 'negative?'

A big part of unhappiness is not knowing who we are and trying to be someone we are not or living a life that does not authentically suit us. This can easily cause a situation where you may feel trapped in patterns, programs, and attachments of trying to be who you think you are 'supposed to be,' and having no idea who you are.

If you don't realize this is happening and learn to listen to your authentic self... an experience of hopelessness, depression, feelings of confusion, powerlessness and even anger can occur.

This week's materials are meant to be an introduction to a better understanding of who you are and who you are not. It is meant to encourage you to learn to listen to yourself and what best fits your life.

To Complete This Week:

1. *7 Days of Identity Insight*: Complete the reflections below for each day starting with day 1

2. *Self-Ratings:*

   a. Rate each day this week, from 1-10 (1 being the least, 10 being the most), on how committed you are to being happy every day.

   b. Identify what zone (red, green, blue or purple zones) your emotions tend to be every day.

   c. Identify where on the *Identity Layers Chart* you are today, "*what layer are you most affected by?*"

3. *Meditations:* Listen to one of the available meditations at least twice this week

4. *Group/Individual Meetings:* Participate in the 3rd individual/group meeting by Zoom or phone

Resources for This Week:

A. Emotion Chart:

PURPLE ZONE: FREEDOM EMOTIONS

*Unity, Big Picture Perspective, Integration, Freedom From 'Self',
Seeing 'Self' in 'Other'*

*Compassion-Based Giving, Balance between 'Self' and 'Other,'
Authenticity, Service, Creativity, Imagination, Faith, Inter-
Dependence, Vision, Empowerment*

*Purpose, Meaning, Mission, Flow State, Connection, Truth, Beauty,
Goals, Wisdom*

BLUE ZONE: UPLIFTING & LIGHTENING EMOTIONS

*Bliss, Serenity, Peace, Harmony, Self-Awareness, Balance
Joy, Enthusiasm, Abundance, Exhilaration, Hope*

*Compassion, Empathy, Inspiration, Clarity, Presence
Love, Appreciation, Gratitude, Devotion, Generosity*

GREEN ZONE: RELIEF EMOTIONS

*Cooperation, Trust, Letting Go, Detachment
Satisfaction, Amusement, Curiosity*

*Power, Strength, Agency, Discovery, Challenge, Discipline
Self-Esteem, Dignity, Duty, Obligation
Neutral, Acceptance, Contentment, Safety
Happy, Excited, Surprised, Fun*

RED ZONE: DESTRUCTIVE & CYCLICAL EMOTIONS

*Anxiety, Nervousness, Shock, Confusion, Control, Stressed, Co-Dependent
Anger, Rage, Avoidance
Guilt, Resentment
Fear, Hatred, Blame, Denial, Self-Centeredness
Sadness, Grief, Loss*

*Isolated, Disconnected, Lonely, Duality
Hopelessness, Resignation, Depression
Powerlessness, Overwhelm, Frozen, Terror, Trauma
Shame, Apathy, Helplessness*

B. Adapted Rational Emotive Behavior Therapy (REBT) Exercises:
-Adapted and simplified by creator of HBM, Sara Spowart, PhD, LMFT

Reframing Negative Beliefs Example:

Negative Identified Belief: *There's no reason to be happy*

What is the benefit of this negatively identified belief?
I get more attention from my family and others when I feel sad

What is the harm of this negatively identified belief?
Feeling bad, not helping mood, or wanting to stay sober

3 Positive Alternatives to Identified Belief:

a. There is at least one reason to be happy

b. Eventually there could be a reason to be happy

c. I am mostly just hurting myself with this belief

C. Identity Layers: Which one are you most affected by?
- Made by HBM creator, Sara Spowart, PhD, LMFT

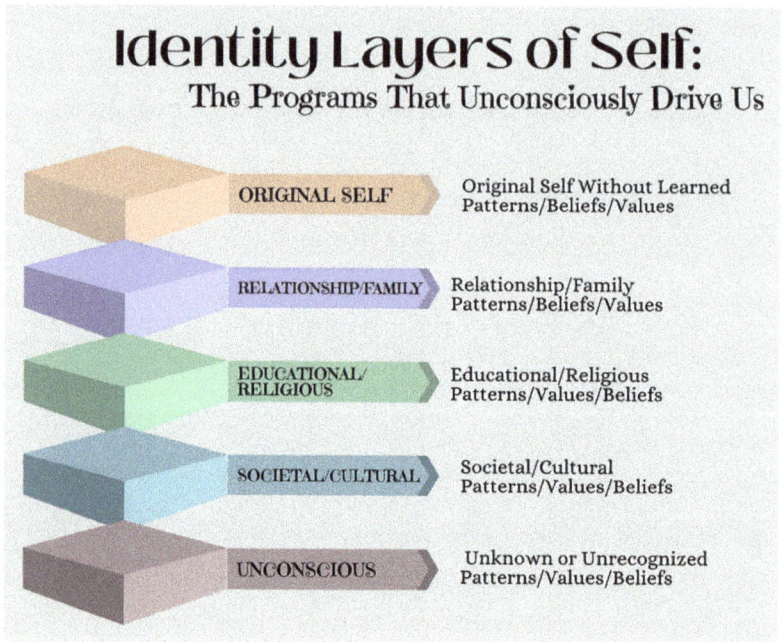

Exercises to complete on your own and then discuss in group/ individual weekly sessions and/or email to the course instructor:

1. **Negative Identified Belief:**

   What is the benefit of this negatively identified belief?

   What is the harm of this negatively identified belief?

   3 Positive Alternatives to Identified Belief:

   a.

b.

c.

2. Negative Identified Belief:

What is the benefit of this negatively identified belief?

What is the harm of this negatively identified belief?

3 Positive Alternatives to Identified Belief:

a.

b.

c.

3. Negative Identified Belief:

What is the benefit of this negatively identified belief?

What is the harm of this negatively identified belief?

3 Positive Alternatives to Identified Belief:

a.

b.

c.

Daily Activities for the Week

Day 1: Week 2

7 Days of Identity Insight: What would be helpful for me to know today? Who Am I? What am I afraid to admit to myself? Please write or do an audio note to reflect

Self-Ratings: Rate, from 1-10 (1 being the least, 10 being the most), how much you loved yourself today.

Self-Ratings: Identify where you mostly were emotionally in the chart today (red, green, blue or purple zones).

Self-Ratings: Identify where on the *Identity Layer Charts* you are today, "*what layer are you most affected by?*"

Day 2: Week 2

7 Days of Identity Insight: What would be helpful for me to know today? Who Am I? What am I afraid to admit to myself? Please write or do an audio note to reflect

Self-Ratings: Rate, from 1-10 (1 being the least, 10 being the most), how much you loved yourself today.

Self-Ratings: Identify where you mostly were emotionally in the chart today (red, green, blue or purple zones).

Self-Ratings: Identify where on the *Identity Layers Chart* you are today, "*what layer are you most affected by?*"

Day 3: Week 2

7 Days of Identity Insight: What would be helpful for me to know today? Who Am I? What am I afraid to admit to myself? Please write or do an audio note to reflect

Self-Ratings: Rate, from 1-10 (1 being the least, 10 being the most), how much you loved yourself today.

Self-Ratings: Identify where you mostly were emotionally in the chart today (red, green, blue or purple zones).

Self-Ratings: Identify where on the *Identity Layers Chart* you are today, "*what are you most affected by?*"

Day 4: Week 2

7 Days of Identity Insight: What would be helpful for me to know today? Who Am I? What am I afraid to admit to myself? Please write or do an audio note to reflect

Self-Ratings: Rate, from 1-10 (1 being the least, 10 being the most), how much you loved yourself today.

Self-Ratings: Identify where you mostly were emotionally in the chart today (red, green, blue or purple zones).

Self-Ratings: Identify where on the *Identity Layers Chart* you are today, "*what layer are you most affected by?*"

Day 5: Week 2

7 Days of Identity Insight: What would be helpful for me to know today? Who Am I? What am I afraid to admit to myself? Please write or do an audio note to reflect

Self-Ratings: Rate, from 1-10 (1 being the least, 10 being the most), how much you loved yourself today.

Self-Ratings: Identify where you mostly were emotionally in the chart today (red, green, or blue zone).

Self-Ratings: Identify where on the *Identity Layers Chart* you are today, "*what layer are you most affected by?*"

Day 6: Week 2

7 Days of Identity Insight: Complete 1-2 adapted REBT exercises. Please write or do an audio note for each

Self-Ratings: Rate, from 1-10 (1 being the least, 10 being the most), how much you loved yourself today.

Self-Ratings: Identify where you mostly were emotionally in the chart today (red, green, blue or purple zones).

Self-Ratings: Identify where on the *Identity Layers Chart* you are today, "*what layer are you most affected by?*"

Day 7: Week 2

7 Days of Identity Insight: Complete 1-2 adapted REBT exercises. Please write or do an audio note for each

Self-Ratings: Rate, from 1-10 (1 being the least, 10 being the most), how much you loved yourself today.

Self-Ratings: Identify where you mostly were emotionally in the chart today (red, green, blue or purple zones).

Self-Ratings: Identify where on the *Identity Layers Chart* you are today, "*what layers are you most affected by?*"

Please participate in either the 30-minute individual or group live compassion-based happiness program on Zoom on Day 7 to reflect, share, process, and have greater support. Please feel free to send your writings/ audio notes from this week to the instructor of the course.

Week 3: Become Your Own Emotional Creator

Seeing beauty/good in the everyday mindfulness- every day take 15 minutes to notice and experience something positive in the blue zone. Know that these things are 'pointers' to the experience and not the experience itself. They are a way of triggering and supporting a positive, uplifting emotion you are trying or wanting to attain. For example, seeing a beautiful tree or park may bring forward feelings of appreciation, peace, calm, and happiness. However, is it the tree and park doing this? Or is it YOU experiencing a positive reaction and interpretation? Does everyone who sees this park/nature feel these emotions or maybe just some?

This week is to help you discover your role and the importance of your role in your happiness and well-being. Yes, of course, certain things may resonate more for certain people. However, it is still coming from you, and it is possible to learn how to increase the experience of certain emotions you would like to have. If you don't know how to do this, another method besides finding things that help to trigger those emotions and then working to cultivate and nurture them…is to *give* the thing you want to experience. This is another way to generate the experience yourself. For example, if you wish you had felt loved as a child by your mother, maybe you can volunteer with children and be loving and nurturing to them. This creates the energy and the emotion you are looking for.

What emotions on the chart are you wanting to experience more of? How have you experienced these in the past and what are the best ways you can increase them now, even in very small ways?

Our habits and patterns of relying on outside things, other people, hopes, dreams, ideas… everything outside of ourselves accepting something inside of ourselves is in itself disempowering and contributes to cycles that individuals can become stuck in with their unhappiness and feeling unable to get out of 'the red zone' or a place of feeling not as good as you know you can feel. Instead of being a victim to certain emotions or patterns, if you could choose how you want to feel like you choose a food item on a menu…what would you want to feel?

During This Week You Will Complete:

1. *Emotional Creator Insights* **daily exercise**

2. *The 3-Day Emotional Creator* **activity**

3. *Meditations* **please listen to one of the available meditations at least twice this week.**

4. *Group/Individual Meetings:* **Please participate in the 4th individual/group meeting by Zoom orphone**

Resources for This Week

A. Emotion Chart

PURPLE ZONE: FREEDOM EMOTIONS

Unity, Big Picture Perspective, Integration, Freedom From 'Self', Seeing 'Self' in 'Other'

Compassion-Based Giving, Balance between 'Self' and 'Other,' Authenticity, Service, Creativity, Imagination, Faith, Inter-Dependence, Vision, Empowerment

Purpose, Meaning, Mission, Flow State, Connection, Truth, Beauty, Goals, Wisdom

BLUE ZONE: UPLIFTING & LIGHTENING EMOTIONS

*Bliss, Serenity, Peace, Harmony, Self-Awareness, Balance
Joy, Enthusiasm, Abundance, Exhilaration, Hope*

*Compassion, Empathy, Inspiration, Clarity, Presence
Love, Appreciation, Gratitude, Devotion, Generosity*

GREEN ZONE: RELIEF EMOTIONS

*Cooperation, Trust, Letting Go, Detachment
Satisfaction, Amusement, Curiosity*

*Power, Strength, Agency, Discovery, Challenge, Discipline
Self-Esteem, Dignity, Duty, Obligation
Neutral, Acceptance, Contentment, Safety
Happy, Excited, Surprised, Fun*

RED ZONE: DESTRUCTIVE & CYCLICAL EMOTIONS

*Anxiety, Nervousness, Shock, Confusion, Control, Stressed, Co-Dependent
Anger, Rage, Avoidance
Guilt, Resentment
Fear, Hatred, Blame, Denial, Self-Centeredness
Sadness, Grief, Loss*

*Isolated, Disconnected, Lonely, Duality
Hopelessness, Resignation, Depression
Powerlessness, Overwhelm, Frozen, Terror, Trauma
Shame, Apathy, Helplessness*

Daily Activity Each Day for 7 Days:

Emotional Creator Insights: What emotions do you tend to create the most? Please reflect on and identify the emotions you tend to be a generator of daily (refer to the chart if/as needed)

Try to be as compassionate, kind, and non-judgmental of yourself as possible. Many of us tend to get stuck in the 'red' zone on the chart, but awareness and mindfulness that we are regularly stuck in the red zone is an important part of getting out of that pattern.

Self-Rating: Please identify where you mostly were emotionally in the chart today (red, green, blue or purple zones).

Day 1: Week 3

Emotional Creator Insights: What emotions do you tend to create most? Please take some time to write or do an audio note on the emotions you tend to create daily (refer to the chart if/as needed).

Self-Rating: Identify where you mostly were emotionally in the chart today (red, green, blue, or purple zones).

Day 2: Week 3

Emotional Creator Insights: What emotions do you tend to create most? Please take some time to write or do an audio note on the emotions you tend to create daily (refer to the chart if/as needed).

Self-Rating: Identify where you mostly were emotionally in the chart today (red, green, blue or purple zones).

Day 3: Week 3

Emotional Creator Insights: What emotions do you tend to create most? Please take some time to write or do an audio note on the emotions you tend to create daily (refer to the chart if/as needed).

Self-Rating: Identify where you mostly were emotionally in the chart today (red, green, blue, or purple zones).

Day 4: Week 3

Emotional Creator Insights: What emotions do you tend to create most? Please take some time to write or do an audio note on the emotions you tend to create daily (refer to the chart if/as needed).

Self-Rating: Identify where you mostly were emotionally in the chart today (red, green, blue, or purple zones).

Day 5: Week 3

Emotional Creator Insights: What emotions do you tend to create most? Please take some time to write or do an audio note on the emotions you tend to create daily (refer to the chart if/as needed).

Self-Rating: Identify where you mostly were emotionally in the chart today (red, green, blue, or purple zones).

Day 6: Week 3

Emotional Creator Insights: What emotions do you tend to create most? Please take some time to write or do an audio note on the emotions you tend to create daily (refer to the chart if/as needed).

Self-Rating: Identify where you mostly were emotionally in the chart today (red, green, blue, or purple zones).

Day 7: Week 3

Emotional Creator Insights: What emotions do you tend to create most? Please take some time to write or do an audio note on the emotions you tend to create daily (refer to the chart if/as needed).

Self-Rating: Identify where you mostly were emotionally in the chart today (red, green, blue or purple zones).

3-Day Emotional Creator Activity

Select 3 Days out of 7 Days in Week 3:

Take out at least 15 timed minutes each day, for 3 different days, and attempt to experience a certain emotion you would like to experience from the chart or something close to that is either in the green zone or the blue zone.

You can use an object or activity to try to initiate these experiences for the first 2 days. Try on the 3rd day to see if you can cultivate that emotion on your own.

For example, if you choose the emotion of peace and serenity... maybe on the first couple of days have a soothing bath with candles, listen to calming music with a cup of tea, and spend time with a pet…whatever is positive for **you**.

After completing the 3 days of green and blue zone 'creator' activities, please reflect on the following:

What emotions are most difficult for you to create in the green or blue zone? Please spend at least 5 minutes writing or making an audio note about the positive emotions that are hardest for you to experience after completing this 3-day activity.

Please participate in either the 30-minute individual or group live compassion-based happiness program on Zoom or phone to reflect, share, process, and have greater support.
Please feel free to send your writings from this week to the instructor of the course.

Week 4: Turning Challenges Into Strengths

One of the traps that can happen with the 'red zone' emotions is not even realizing you are experiencing them and are stuck in repetitive patterns and reactivity within them. Weeks 1-3 were focused on creating awareness of patterns you may be stuck in, your general emotional tendencies and habits, and decided to intentionally create the emotions you would like to experience and focus more on that. In Week 4 we look at how we can shift and change painful thoughts, feelings, and experiences into something positive. Suffering happens to everyone at some point and in different forms. However, it is possible to turn trauma, pain, and 'red zone' emotions into something that benefits yourself and others when seen from different vantage points.

Turning painful things into strengths is not meant to invalidate the destructive, challenging emotions and experiences you have had. Rather, it is meant to help empower you to take back some control over your life and move forward from the experience. It is a way of redefining what has happened in your past or present so that you can see yourself and the negative emotions through a new lens, and make something constructive from it.

During This Week You Will Complete:

1. *3 Days of Transformation* to shift negative 'red zone' emotions into 'green' or 'blue' zone emotions. Please complete the reflections below for each day starting with Day 1.

2. Please identify *at least one moment* you experienced in the blue zone (of the emotion chart) each day. *Which emotion in the blue zone did you experience in this/thesemoment/s?*

3. Please listen to one of the available meditations provided in the program at least twice this week.

4. *Group/Individual Meetings:* Please participate in the 5th individual/group meeting by Zoom or phone this week

3 Days of Transformation (Choose any 3 days out of the 7) this week to complete:

Day 1: Week 4

Please reflect on the term "radical acceptance." What does this mean to you? What are some things you have already been able to accept that were difficult in your life?

Please write or do an audio note for each question

Day 2: Week 4

Please write or do an audio note on a negative emotion you have been struggling with such as guilt, anxiety, depression, stress, or shame.

Please consider thanking it for what it has done in your life, the negative and positive things it has brought you, and telling it kindly that you no longer need it and are ready to let it go and to live in greater harmony and acceptance of it.

Day 3: Week 4

Please reflect on 3 things in your life that have upset you or you felt were negative and or harmful from your past. Below, please write each one out, and reflect on a strength you've gained or potential positive that can come from each painful thing. Lastly, please consider thanking each panful thing for the role it has served in your life and any positive that has come or could eventually come from it.

a.

b.

c.

Daily Activity Each Day for 7 Days:

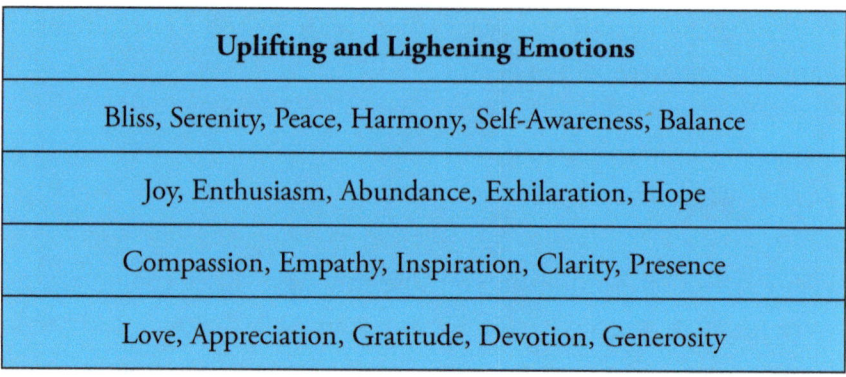

Uplifting and Lighening Emotions
Bliss, Serenity, Peace, Harmony, Self-Awareness, Balance
Joy, Enthusiasm, Abundance, Exhilaration, Hope
Compassion, Empathy, Inspiration, Clarity, Presence
Love, Appreciation, Gratitude, Devotion, Generosity

Please identify *at least one moment* you experienced in the blue zone (of the emotion chart) each day this week. Which emotion in the blue zone did you experience in this/these moment/s?

Day 1:

Day 2:

Day 3:

Day 4:

Day 5:

Day 6:

Day 7:

Week 5: Taking Responsibility for Your Happiness

One of the great challenges with happiness is the transition from being in the red zone of negative emotions and/or feeling like a victim to feeling we have more power and control over ourselves and can make some small steps (or even big ones) toward more positive emotions and feeling we have more agency and influence over our internal state of being. We may not always even be able to change our outer circumstances at all or very much, but we can work to internally feel better. This is a great act of self-kindness, self-love, and compassion for ourselves when we feel stuck. It is acknowledging that you love yourself enough that you want to feel better now, even if it takes time for outer circumstances to change. Oftentimes destructive emotions like anger, anxiety, stress, guilt, shame, and hopelessness, tend to create more and more of those emotional experiences. By starting from a better feeling state and focusing on increasing that, you are not invalidating your negative experiences…rather you are saying you are valuable enough that you deserve to feel better no matter what has occurred.

This week we will be learning and focusing on activities to help with increasing individual agency, empowerment, and accountability in our lived experience with happiness. This does not mean everything will bring joy from the outside. However, it means we can work to create an internal state of happiness and well-being, regardless of challenging outside circumstances.

During This Week You Will Complete:

1. *7-Day Happiness Challenge*: Please complete the reflections below for each day starting with Day 1

2. *Self-Ratings*: Please rate each day this week, from 1-10 (1 being the least, 10 being the most), how committed you are to being happy every day

3. *7 Days of Simplification*: Please engage in one simplification activity each day this week. Simplification refers to small ways you can reduce stress, unnecessary busyness, addiction to activity, and discomfort with having little to do and stillness.

4. *Meditations:* Please listen to one of the available meditations at least three times this week

5. *Group/Individual Meetings:* Please participate in the 6th individual/group meeting by Zoom or phone

Day 1: Week 5

7 Days of Happiness Challenge: What does it mean to you to be happy? How committed do you feel to being happy? Please write or do an audio note for each question

Self-Ratings: Please rate, from 1-10 (1 being the least, 10 being the most), how committed you were to being happy today.

7 Days of Simplification: Please find one thing or thought you can cut down on that would help simplify your life more.

Day 2: Week 5

7 Days of Happiness Challenge: What does it mean to you to be unhappy? How committed do you feel to being unhappy? Please write or do an audio note for each question

Self-Ratings: Please rate, from 1-10 (1 being the least, 10 being the most), how committed you were to being happy today.

7 Days of Simplification: Please find one thing or thought you can cut down on that would help simplify your life more.

Day 3: Week 5

7 Days of Happiness Challenge: How responsible do you feel you are for your happiness? What is the role that other people, places, and situations play in your happiness? Please write or do an audio note for each question

Self-Ratings: Please rate, from 1-10 (1 being the least, 10 being the most), how committed you were to being happy today.

7 Days of Simplification: Please find one thing or thought you can cut down on that would help simplify your life more.

Day 4: Week 5

7 Days of Happiness Challenge: Is it self-loving and kind to yourself to be happy? Is it self-loving and kind to yourself to be unhappy? What are the benefits and negatives of both?
Please write or do an audio note for each question

Self-Ratings: Please rate, from 1-10 (1 being the least, 10 being the most), how committed you were to being happy today.

7 Days of Simplification: Please find one thing or thought you can cut down on that would help simplify your life more.

Day 5: Week 5

7 Days of Happiness Challenge: What role does the decision to be happy or unhappy play in someone's well-being? Is it possible to decide to be happy no matter what and stick to this.... or is this unrealistic and too optimistic? Please write or do an audio note for each question

Self-Ratings: Please rate, from 1-10 (1 being the least, 10 being the most), how committed you were to being happy today.

7 Days of Simplification: Please find one thing or thought you can cut down on that would help simplify your life more.

Day 6: Week 5

7 Days of Happiness Challenge: What are some benefits that some-one might perceive they have from feeling angry, upset, and unhappy? Please write or do an audio note for each question

Self-Ratings: Please rate, from 1-10 (1 being the least, 10 being the most), how committed you were to being happy today.

7 Days of Simplification: Please find one thing or thought you can cut down on that would help simplify your life more.

Day 7: Week 5

7 Days of Happiness Challenge: How can I take better care of myself? How can I show myself more love and compassion every day? Please write or do an audio note for each question

Self-Ratings: Please rate, from 1-10 (1 being the least, 10 being the most), how committed you were to being happy today.

7 Days of Simplification: Please find one thing or thought you can cut down on that would help simplify your life more.

Week 6: Living and Loving Our Life and Ourselves on Purpose

There is value in living our lives 'on purpose,' or with intentionality. Creating intentions for ourselves, our families, communities, relationships, and how we want to contribute and engage with ourselves and others is important for one's happiness. Instead of living in a reactionary manner, or a manner habituated by patterns and norms, it is valuable to think about being aware and deciding how you want to experience your inner world and working towards that goal. We exist in systems within ourselves, our families, communities, societies, and cultures (and more). Therefore, individuals exist within systems that are connected directly and indirectly with others. An analogy could be with a fish bowl full of fish. Whatever one fish does, indirectly impacts the whole fish bowl.

Therefore, there is value in kindness towards yourself and towards others; and there is value in being happy, feeling hopeful, and inspired. It not only helps you with your own mental, emotional, physical, and relational health…but positively impacts those indirectly or directly associated with you.

This week we will be working on the topic of increasing and maintaining conscious kindness, as well as increasing your level of inspiration and motivation about your sense of purpose and your life. We will also be exploring ways to take the skills learned from this course and implement them in a more manageable, long-term manner.

During This Week You Will Complete:

1. *7 Days of Kindness* to help increase levels of happiness and move yourself more often into the 'green' and 'blue' zone emotions.

2. *Increase Your Inspiration:* please complete the prompts below to increase insight and improve motivation and inspiration.

3. *Meditations:* Please listen to one of the available meditations provided in the program at least three times this week.

4. *Group/Individual Meetings:* Please participate in the 7th individual/group meeting by Zoom or phone

Day 1: Week 6

7 Days of Kindness: Think of two causes you might care about that are happening either in your community, the country, or the world. Please write or do an audio note about each.

a.

b.

Increase Your Inspiration: Is there anything you'd like to do or experience in your life that you haven't done yet? Please write or do an audio note

Day 2: Week 6

7 Days of Kindness: Please intentionally do one act of kindness for yourself or someone else today.

7 Days of Kindness: Please read these phrases and select one (or create one) that feels most supportive for you.

I am committed to being happy and healthy no matter what
I am inherently valuable no matter what
My life is improving every day
I always make small, baby steps towards a better future
I care about myself and how I feel
I experience positive emotions every day
I am thankful for my life and experience positive emotion

Increase Your Inspiration: What does it mean to feel inspired to you? What helps you to know you are inspired? Please reflect and write out or do an audio note on your thoughts of what inspires and motivates you

Day 3: Week 6

7 Days of Kindness: Please intentionally do one act of kindness for yourself or someone else today.

7 Days of Kindness: Please read these phrases and select one (or create one) that feels most supportive for you.

I always make choices to help increase my happiness
I love myself unconditionally
I care about myself and how I feel

Increase Your Inspiration: Please intentionally find something that makes you laugh today.

Day 4: Week 6

Increase Your Inspiration: Part of happiness is not only attaining things we think we want or need; it may also be the experience of positive emotions and relief from negative emotions that can exist as an internal state, regardless of current life circumstances. Please reflect on this and write about it for at least 5 minutes

7 Days of Kindness: Please intentionally do one act of kindness for yourself or someone else today.

Day 5: Week 6

Increase Your Inspiration: How has your perception of happiness changed during this program? Please write or do any audio notes on each question

Increase Your Inspiration: How worthwhile is it to focus on increasing happiness in your life? Why might it make a difference? Please write or do any audio notes on each question

7 Days of Kindness: Please intentionally do one act of kindness for yourself or someone else today.

Day 6: Week 6

Increase Your Inspiration: What 'blue zone' emotions will you strive to integrate into your everyday life going forward beyond this program? How will you maintain your commitment to continue to implement this? Please write or do any audio notes on each question

7 Days of Kindness: Please intentionally do one act of kindness for yourself or someone else today.

Day 7: Week 6

Increase Your Inspiration: What is a takeaway you would like to share with others who take this course in the future or with current participants? What do you feel has changed about yourself, if anything, throughout this course? Please write or do an audio note

7 Days of Kindness: Please intentionally do one act of kindness for yourself or someone else today.

For Instructors of Happiness-Based Mindfulness:

1. **Participate in the initial training meeting and review the program, core concepts, course set-up, and activities.**

2. **Please complete Happiness-Based Mindfulness over 6 sessions in total. Completing the program will help you to be ready to teach so you are familiar with and have a deep understanding of the material.**

3. **Please read and reference the required materials listed below on topics that will be important for reflection and discussion from participants. These include an understanding of the concept of radical acceptance, mindfulness for happiness, reframing negative beliefs and thoughts, mindfulness in everyday life for improvement of emotions, and self-kindness.**

Required Reading Materials for Instructors in Training: Provided Through Accompanying PDFs for Instructors in Training

Hook, J. N., Hodge, A. S., Zhang, H., Van Tongeren, D. R., & Davis, D. E. (2023). Minimalism,voluntary simplicity, and well-being: A systematic review of the empirical literature. *The Journal of Positive Psychology*, *18*(1), 130-141.

Honmore, V. M. (2023). Mindfulness, Happiness and Well-being among Adults. *Indian Journal of Positive Psychology*, *14*(2), 184–187.

Rowland, L., & Curry, O. S. (2019). A range of kindness activities boosts happiness. *The Journal of Social Psychology*, *159*(3), 340-343.

Segal. (2023). Does acceptance lead to change? Training in radical acceptance improves the implementation of cognitive reappraisal. *Behavior Research and Therapy. 164.*

Happiness–Based Mindfulness Approach: The A-Zs of Happiness

A 12-Week Intensive

A Literary Accompaniment to the book *You Are Love: The Discovery of Happiness*

Created By:
Sara Spowart, PhD, DMFT, LMFT, MPA, MA, RYT, CC.Ht.

Author's Note

I wanted to create a mental health psychoeducation program that could be applied practically, in an easy-to-replicate way, to help almost anyone, and provide concrete tools that support overview concepts from my book "You Are Love: The Discovery of Happiness." Happiness-Based Mindfulness is the result. There are three versions of Happiness-Based Mindfulness. One version is a 3-session approach and is more oriented towards trauma and compassion-based psychoeducational tools. A second version is a 6-week program and provides a general overview and application of Happiness-Based Mindfulness core concepts and their meaning. It provides the fundamental tools from the program and their general application to your state of current and future life circumstances. The third version is the 12-week intensive that goes into depth with the A-Zs of happiness, as delineated by the author of Happiness-Based Mindfulness. The 12-week intensive Happiness-Based Mindfulness Approach is provided here. The 12-module version is 12 weeks in length and includes weekly zoom meetings that can be conducted either individually or for a group. These three versions of Happiness-Based Mindfulness, like my book "You Are Love: The Discovery of Happiness," are the representation of my hope to provide information in a practical, feasible way to sustainably improve happiness for anyone who makes use of this.

Wishing you so much happiness, joy, peace, love, kindness, and the feeling of total and complete, integrated wholeness <3

Overview of the HBM

Happiness-Based Mindfulness is designed to help improve the lived experience of happiness in your everyday life. It contains twelve modules and incorporates key components of happiness and well-being in every module. These modules include practical tools that can be implemented in everyday life. In this program, the term 'happiness' means a state of contentment and satisfaction regardless of one's situation. Happiness may be experienced as a temporary state, but aspects that comprise happiness like a sense of purpose, connection, meaning, and working towards a higher purpose are more stable and long-lasting.

The 12 modules include recurring key components. These include 1) understanding your identity structure and assessing what you want it to be instead of accepting already prescribed programs; 2) understanding any loops or patterns you may feel trapped in and how to get out; 3) an understanding of how we are generators of emotion and how to take our power back and the energy we want to generate; 4) bringing awareness to our levels of happiness regularly as a method to increase well-being; 5) accountability and responsibility for your lived experience of happiness and what you would like to change or accept; 6) bringing more love and kindness into your life as a method to increase your happiness; 7) connection as a means of sustainable happiness. These concepts are implemented in practical, easy-to-understand ways throughout the course with weekly meetings, hypnotherapy meditations, and daily exercises.

Let's get started! :)

The A-Zs of Happiness in Happiness-Based Mindfulness (HBM)

A. Emotion Chart

PURPLE ZONE: FREEDOM EMOTIONS

Unity, Big Picture Perspective, Integration, Freedom From 'Self', Seeing 'Self' in 'Other'

Compassion-Based Giving, Balance between 'Self' and 'Other,' Authenticity, Service, Creativity, Imagination, Faith, Inter-Dependence, Vision, Empowerment

Purpose, Meaning, Mission, Flow State, Connection, Truth, Beauty, Goals, Wisdom

BLUE ZONE: UPLIFTING & LIGHTENING EMOTIONS

Bliss, Serenity, Peace, Harmony, Self-Awareness, Balance
Joy, Enthusiasm, Abundance, Exhilaration, Hope

Compassion, Empathy, Inspiration, Clarity, Presence
Love, Appreciation, Gratitude, Devotion, Generosity

GREEN ZONE: RELIEF EMOTIONS

Cooperation, Trust, Letting Go, Detachment
Satisfaction, Amusement, Curiosity

Power, Strength, Agency, Discovery, Challenge, Discipline
Self-Esteem, Dignity, Duty, Obligation
Neutral, Acceptance, Contentment, Safety
Happy, Excited, Surprised, Fun

RED ZONE: DESTRUCTIVE & CYCLICAL EMOTIONS

Anxiety, Nervousness, Shock, Confusion, Control, Stressed, Co-Dependent
Anger, Rage, Avoidance
Guilt, Resentment
Fear, Hatred, Blame, Denial, Self-Centeredness
Sadness, Grief, Loss

Isolated, Disconnected, Lonely, Duality
Hopelessness, Resignation, Depression
Powerlessness, Overwhelm, Frozen, Terror, Trauma
Shame, Apathy, Helplessness

B. Schedule of Zoom or Phone Meetings for 12-Week Course

Please be prepared to set aside approximately a total of 3 hours a week over the next 12 weeks for the successful completion of this course

Week 1	Program & Resource Overview 1st Day of Week 1 (30 Minute Meeting)
Week 1	7th Day of Week 1 (30 Minute Meeting)
Week 2	7th Day of Week 2 (30 Minute Meeting)
Week 3	7th Day of Week 3 (30 Minute Meeting)
Week 4	7th Day of Week 4 (30 Minute Meeting)
Week 5	7th Day of Week 5 (30 Minute Meeting)
Week 6	7th Day of Week 6 (30 Minute Meeting)
Week 7	7th Day of Week 7 (30 Minute Meeting)
Week 8	7th Day of Week 8 (30 Minute Meeting)
Week 9	7th Day of Week 9 (30 Minute Meeting)
Week 10	7th Day of Week 10 (30 Minute Meeting)

Week 11	7th Day of Week 11 (30 Minute Meeting)
Week 12	7th Day of Week 12 (30 Minute Meeting)

C. 21 Hypnotherapy Meditations for Happiness-Based Mindfulness
   - *Created by HBM creator Sara Spowart, Ph.D., LMFT*

1. **Authentic-Self Hypnotherapy Meditation**

2. **Beauty Hypnotherapy Meditation**

3. **Dissociation Hypnotherapy Meditation**

4. **General Hypnotherapy Meditation**

5. **Happy Relationship Hypnotherapy Meditation**

6. **Health Hypnotherapy Meditation**

7. **Safety Hypnotherapy Meditation**

8. **Self-Worth and Confidence Hypnotherapy Meditation**

9. **Sleep Hypnotherapy Meditation**

10. **Stress and Calm Hypnotherapy Meditation**

11. **Success Hypnotherapy Meditation**

12. **Wealth Hypnotherapy Meditation**

13. **Happiness Hypnotherapy Meditation**

14. **Freedom and Ease Hypnotherapy Meditation**

15. **Worry and Presence Hypnotherapy Meditation**

16. **Money Hypnotherapy Meditation**

17. **Healing Childhood Trauma and Abuse Hypnotherapy Meditation**

18. **Healing from Trauma Hypnotherapy Meditation**

19. **Increasing Hope, Inspiration and Positive Energy Hypnotherapy Meditation**

20. **Future Full Potential Self Hypnotherapy Meditation**

21. **Rest Hypnotherapy Meditation**

D. **Identity Layers Chart: Which are you most affected by?**
   - Created by Sara Spowart, Ph.D., LMFT

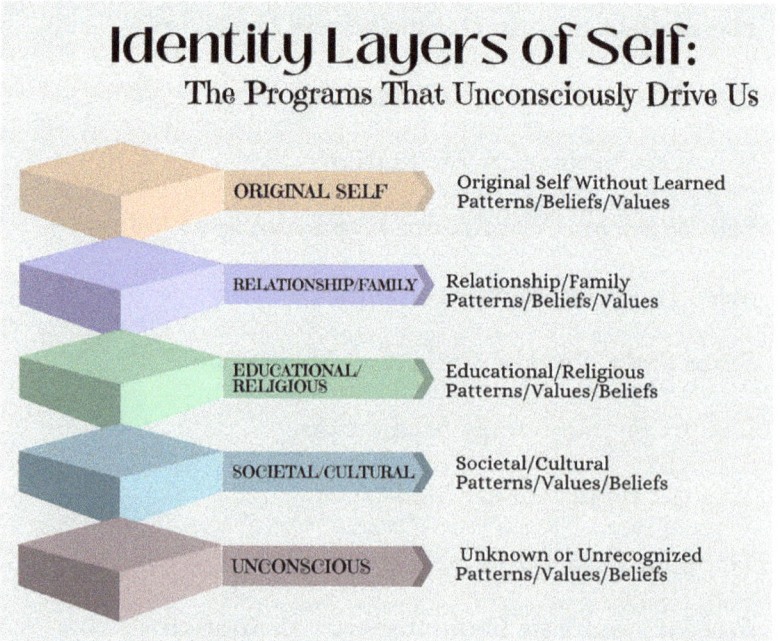

E. Trapped Cycles

- Created by Sara Spowart, Ph.D., LMFT

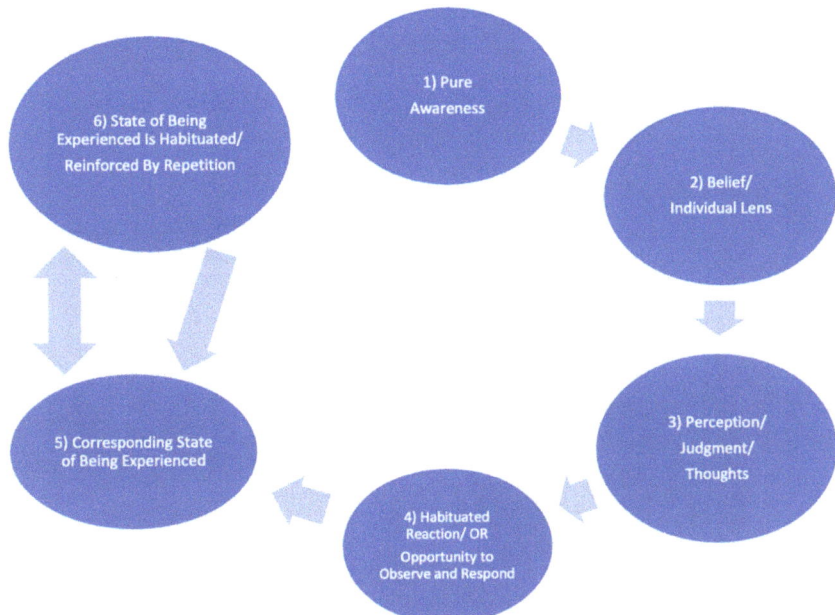

F. Where are you? The Present or Somewhere Else?
 - Created by Sara Spowart, Ph.D., LMFT

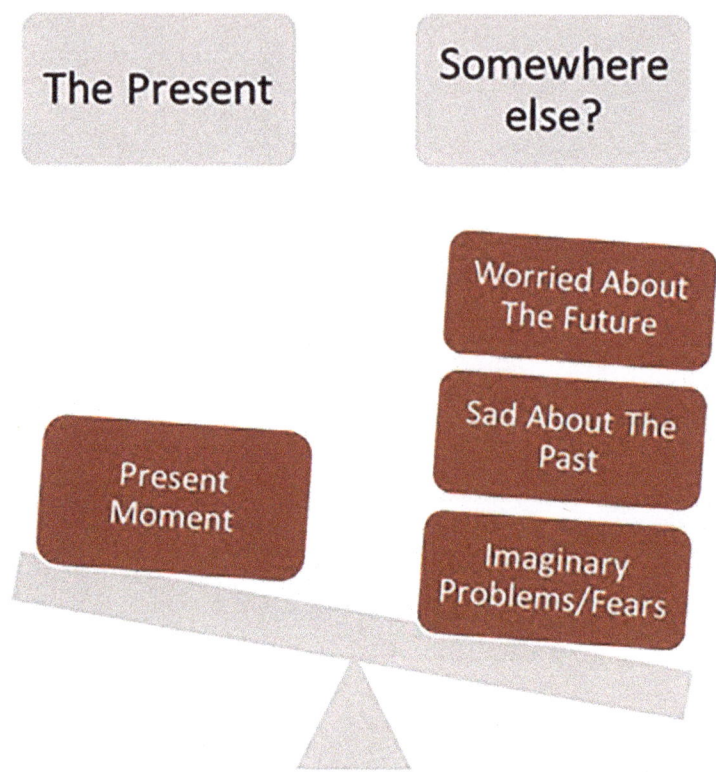

G. Adapted REBT Exercises
 - Adapted by Sara Spowart, Ph.D., LMFT

1. Negative Identified Belief:

What is the benefit of this negatively identified belief?

What is the harm of this negatively identified belief?

3 Positive Alternatives to Identified Belief:

a.

b.

c.

H. Love and Awareness Charts
Created by Sara Spowart, Ph.D., LMFT

Self-Love Chart

Love Myself Unconditionally
Love Myself
Like Myself
Neutral about Myself
Don't Like Myself
Hate Myself
Don't Understand or Know What This Means
Unconscious Reactions, Habits, and Patterns

Other-Love Chart

Love Others Unconditionally
Love Others
Like Others
Neutral about Others
Don't Like Others
Hate Others
Don't Understand or Know What This Means
Unconscious Reactions, Habits, and Patterns

I. Hope Spectrum

- Created by Sara Spowart, Ph.D., LMFT

Toxic Hope (Delusional Hope/Toxic Positivity)
Unhealthy Levels of Hope (Delusional positive levels of hope, and as a result stay in abusive, unhealthy, or painful situations)
Healthy Hope (Acknowledgement of reality and current situation, compassion for levels of suffering, and ability to form hopeful ideas for the future)
Unhealthy Levels of Hope (Insufficient hope levels and sadness, anxiety, and depression as a result)
Toxic Hope (Lack of Hope/Overly Negative Hopelessness)

J. Mirror of Self
- Created by Sara Spowart, Ph.D., LMFT

Mirror of Self. Spend a minimum of at least 1 minute, non-judgmentally looking at yourself in the mirror today, without distractions. Identify where you were on the Mirror of Self-activity each day

(*Authentic Living, Healthy Narcissism, living by 'Shoulds', Playing Roles, Wearing a Mask, Unhealthy Narcissism*).

Day 1:

Day 2:

Day 3:

Day 4:

Day 5:

Day 6:

Day 7:

K. Bird's Eye View Exercise
- Created by Sara Spowart, Ph.D., LMFT

Bird's Eye View Activity: Imagine each day the perspective of at least one other person in your life. What would it be like to experience their emotions, thoughts, and physical sensations? What would life be like through their eyes for just 1 minute today? Try to reflect that we may all have our perspective of our everyday life and circumstances, and all see from different vantage points.

How can you bring compassion, empathy, or detachment into your experiences when working to see through another person's eyes? We tend to project our thoughts, feelings, ideas, and perceptions onto others (both positive and negative). Can we detach from those projections, and see clearly who others are?

Partner/Close Friends?

Work Colleagues/Boss?

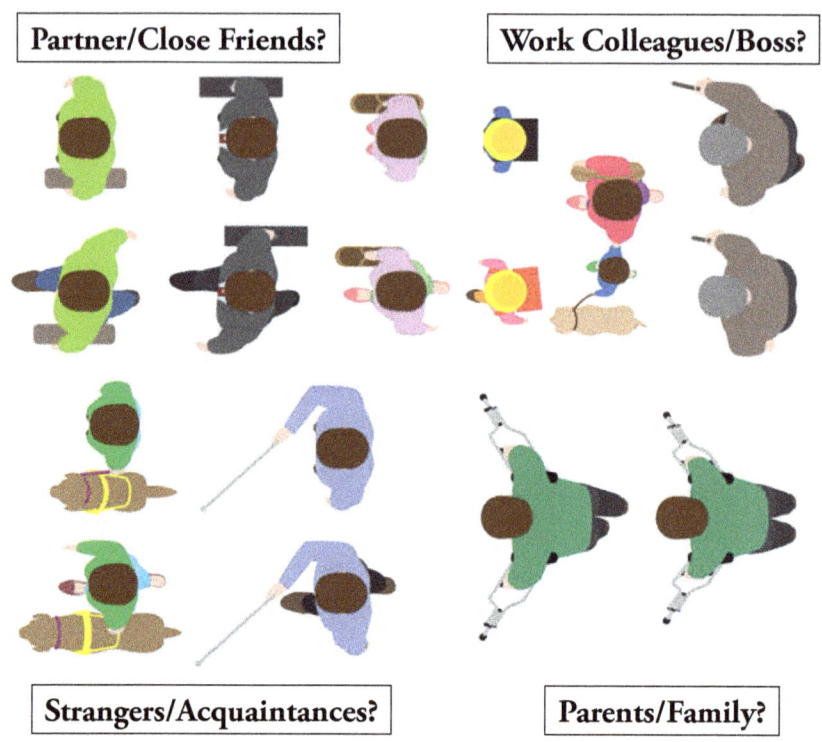

Strangers/Acquaintances?

Parents/Family?

L. Future Jumping Exercise

- Created by Sara Spowart, Ph.D., LMFT

Visual for 2 minutes each day the 'future you' 1 year from now. Where are you going? How is it different from the current you? What advice would this future you have for you that you can bring into the now?

M. Body Love Exercise
- Created by Sara Spowart, Ph.D., LMFT

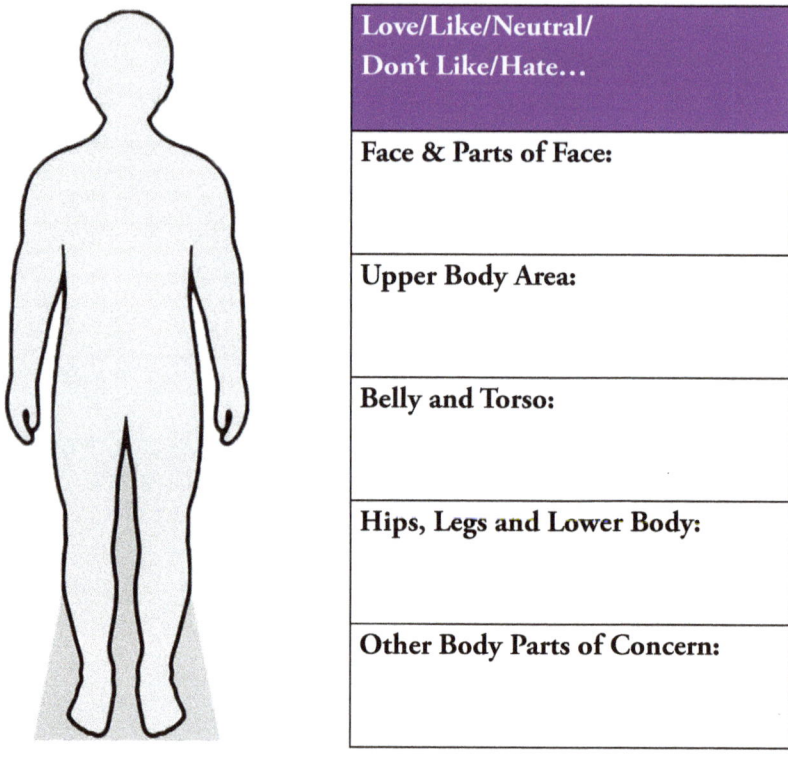

Love/Like/Neutral/ Don't Like/Hate…
Face & Parts of Face:
Upper Body Area:
Belly and Torso:
Hips, Legs and Lower Body:
Other Body Parts of Concern:

Identify *how you felt about your body* each day this week. Please refer to the Body Love Image.

Day 1:

Day 2:

Day 3:

Day 4:

Day 5:

Day 6:

Day 7:

N. Gratitude/Manifestation and Fear Exercise

This is a simple but powerful exercise. I find that many people think gratitude and appreciation mean being happy about things they are not happy about. Or they must accept and be ok with whatever causes them great pain and suffering. However, this unique appreciation activity involves having a 'happy partner.' With this happiness partner, send each other messages or journal entries on what you are feeling afraid about and what you have an appreciation for. With these messages, the gratitude and appreciation of your journal do not have to be things that have happened yet. It refers to things that have maybe happened, but also things you would like to happen. You will find that each day as you do this, the fears will decrease, and the feeling of possibility and clarity on what you want will increase. You can also do this by sending an email to the facilitator of the class every day or keeping a journal. However, an important part of progress and positive changes in mindset is to share the fears as well as what you are manifesting into gratitude in your life or the lives of others. Don't keep it to yourself, it needs to be expressed for this exercise to have the greatest positive impact. If you have resistance or fear about sharing, this might also be an important edge to explore and better understand.

So, in both in manifested and yet to be manifested form…

1. *What are you feeling appreciative of today?*

2. *What are you afraid about today?*

Example:

Appreciation/Manifested Appreciation: I am so appreciative today for the $50 million grant I received to help bring greater happiness, kindness, and love into the world! I am so happy and appreciative because I bought a house today!

My Fears: I am afraid I will never have a healthy body or get strong and in shape.

O. Duality Exercises

- Created by Sara Spowart, Ph.D., LMFT

This …
That …
This AND That.

Journal in 4-7 sentences something that you are struggling with and seems to be dualistic, but maybe could be 'this' AND 'that.' What are areas of your life that have caused pain, difficulty, and stress thinking there is only 'this' or 'that' but not 'this and that?'

What is the benefit of thinking it's 'this' or 'that'? What is the benefit of considering the thing you are struggling with has more than one 'right' answer, or more than one 'wrong' answer?

Can you abide by this ambiguity?

A major part of happiness is feeling a sense of wholeness, completeness, and integration. When we feel that 1) our lives are being lived in duality, 2) there are different parts to ourselves or conflicting beliefs and understanding, or 3) we try to push a perspective of sameness without integrating the parts…we suffer greatly. Integration and wholeness mean we become more and more at peace with all aspects of ourselves and the world around us. Maybe happiness is more about integration, and less about judging, dividing, and separating.

P. Always Feel Connected Rating
- Created by Sara Spowart, Ph.D., LMFT

One of the greatest challenges with happiness can be the modern-day phenomenon of feeling isolated, disconnected, alone, and depressed. We are meant to feel connected and part of something larger than ourselves. When we feel separate, isolated, cut off, and empty…it can be a type of metaphoric hell. This is why it is so important to experience a sense of connection and interconnectedness with something greater than ourselves. This can be connected with pets, nature, family, friends, a higher power, a passion, helping others, being of service, etc. What helps you to feel connected?

What we measure we tend to improve. Therefore, to feel more connected, it is worthwhile to first develop a practice of measuring how connected you feel each day. This will help bring awareness to your level and experience of connection, as well as how to improve it.

Everyday rate how *connected* you feel from 0-10
(0 is not at all connected and 10 is completely connected)

Q. Kindness Rating
- Created by Sara Spowart, Ph.D., LMFT

A key factor in happiness is kindness towards yourself and others. This kindness is generally improved through mindfulness and cultivating awareness of our level of kindness to ourselves and others. The more we practice kindness to ourselves and others, the better we feel about ourselves, and the more our self-esteem is improved. Having positive self-esteem is a key part of happiness. If we feel bad about ourselves, it is hard to be happy, hopeful, or positive. Therefore, practicing kindness is an often, under-utilized happiness improvement approach.

What we measure we tend to improve. This exercise is meant to help improve our levels of happiness by measuring the kindness we are experiencing and expressing in our everyday lives.

How *kind are you being to yourself* today from 0-10? ("0" being the least and "10" being the most)

How *kind are you being to others* today from 0-10? ("0" being the least and "10" being the most)

R. Clinging or Detached? *The Chart of Intention*
- *Created by Sara Spowart, Ph.D., LMFT*

At the core of most suffering is the experience that we may be clinging through attachment to what we are afraid to lose or what we
think or feel we need to do, have, be, or experience to 1) survive, 2)
be happy, 3) experience as little pain and as much pleasure as possible. At the root of much of our behavior is the tendency to push
away and reject what we think will cause pain and to go towards and
possibly hold onto or cling to that which we think will provide the
greatest pleasure, comfort, and happiness. Most of our clinging, inse-
cure attachment, anxiety, and fear over loss come from low tolerance
or intolerance to distress and pain.

Essentially, as humans, we generally don't like pain and do everything possible to avoid it. But at the same time, we cause ourselves
distress, anxiety, and pain through the fear of loss and clinging or
trying to control what we think is good. This push and pull can be
very egoistic, painful, and also controlling. In reality, there is more

going on than we can imagine and we can't know what will be the best for us. Who can say in the end what is good or bad? Maybe some of the worst, most painful things in your life have led to significant and incredible positives you hadn't anticipated before. Maybe our evolution and growth are more important than feeling comfortable, and content and experiencing our pleasure. Our greatest growth may come from stretching ourselves and our expansion rather than clinging or excessively attaching to what feels most comfortable.

What role does detachment play in this? Well with detachment it does not mean you don't care. Rather it means you pull your energy back, like an energy ball that has been radiating out everywhere to many people, ideas, and situations. You bring it back so you can claim it for how you choose to experience or express it. Would you like to experience yourself as an energy ball of love, of peace, of joy? You get to choose. Detachment means instead of living in fear of loss, trying to anxiously push certain outcomes or hold onto things you feel are yours, or spreading your energy thin in many directions and situations…you claim and orient it through your will and intention. You live through clear intention instead of reactive emotion.

Chart of Intention

Fully Aware of My Energy State and Living with Clear Intention
Partially Aware of My Energy State and Living Partially with Intention and Partially through Reaction and fear of loss or change
Not aware of energy state and not living with intention, living through fear of loss or change and with reaction to what is perceived as pleasurable or painful

S. Service

"The highest form of love is service"

"The highest form of love is service." One of the fastest ways to feel and be happier is to live a service life. By providing service to others, care, and concern, we go beyond the focus on the small "I" and expand our awareness outward to something greater. Service is a way to apply love, or engage in practical love.

You don't need to wait until you feel you're in 'the perfect state' to practice service and do something to help others more. It is a misconception to see the world in this way, because most likely that 'perfect state' will be short-lived or never come. Rather, it is better to understand that you can find a way to increase your levels of energy and well-being by acting in a state of service. You will not deplete yourself working through service, you will improve your self-esteem, and how much you value yourself, and help get out of self-centered repetitive patterns and loops. Service also brings a new energetic pattern to engage yourself in. Instead of old patterns and loops, you are getting out of your head and into awareness that there is more than just you, and more than the usual things you are worried or distracted about.

So, what are some ways you can act in service? Maybe you could offer to help someone every day, like an intentional act of kindness? Or you can donate your time or money to a cause you care about? It doesn't have to be big; it could be just $5 a month that you donate, or 1 hour a month. In the end, even though it might seem you are doing it for others because we are all so interconnected, you are ultimately helping yourself. Being of service and giving is one of the fastest ways to feel wealthier, healthier, happier, more energetic, and full of empowered hope. However, it's also something very few people are intentionally practicing.

Although it is not a popular or common idea, there is increasing evidence that things like being of service, volunteering, and thinking of others all help YOU and how you feel. This is not referring to detrimental or imbalance giving...all things need to be done in a state of balance. However, you don't need to wait for the 'perfect' time to help or when you have everything you think you want or need to help. You can do something small to help today.

Like getting yourself into better physical shape, it is hard at first to start working out. Similarly, if you've been on a steady mental diet of self-centeredness, feeling like a victim, or that you can barely handle life...this idea of service might seem like being asked to move mountains. However, this is not the case. In reality, any change (no matter how small) in the momentum of our energetic habits, patterns, and lifestyles can seem daunting, uncomfortable, and even painful at first. Yet, with commitment and discipline, you can shift into new patterns and habits. It is a societal misconception that self-centeredness is the key to success and happiness. Self-centeredness is effective for short-term happiness in certain situations. However, it is ineffective for sustainable happiness.

Self-centeredness tends to create patterns of chronic or subtle discontent and wanting more; as well as dissatisfaction with what you have and entitlement for more. Therefore, instead of seeing the world through the lens of "I don't have enough," "I am a victim," or "I, I, I..." try to see the bigger picture. We are inherently tribal, community-oriented, highly interconnected beings. By giving something, no matter how small it is, to others, you will start to feel better, about yourself.

Service Rating Activity
- Created by Sara Spowart, Ph.D., LMFT

The Service Rating Activity works to help you improve your awareness and level of service. It is an applied mindfulness activity. When we measure something, we tend to improve it and become more aware of it.

How *much are you in authentic service* today from 0-10? ("0" being not at all, and "10" being the most possible)

T. Emotion Creator Activity

- Created by Sara Spowart, Ph.D., LMFT

We are major creators of our own emotions. However, when we are caught up in states of reactivity, joy, or pain, we can lose ourselves in those states or try to cling to them or run away from them. However, we don't often realize we are the source of those emotional states to begin with. For example, have you ever looked at a puppy and felt love for that puppy? Is the love coming from you, or the puppy? Probably from you, the puppy doesn't know what's going on. The same could be true for a young baby. This is just a tangible way to understand that much of what we feel and experience may be largely coming from us. Love for your children, or disdain for them…is probably coming from you and out to others. Individuals who are experiencing a lot of suffering and pain demonstrate this, by being so filled up with pain that it flows out from them and onto others. They are the creators of their pain, and that pain flows out through them.

In the Emotional Creator Activity, we try to bring consciousness to your states of being and what emotional states you may be generating (or creating) yourself, but are caught up in and unaware of your role. By facilitating awareness of your state of being…you can become more conscious and intentional regarding where you want to give your focus and attention as it concerns your happiness.

For this activity, take out at least 15 minutes each day, for 3 different days over a week, and attempt to intentionally create a certain emotion you'd like to experience. You can use an object or activity to attempt to initiate these experiences for the first 2 days. On the 3rd day, try to see if you can cultivate that emotion on your own. For example, if you choose the emotion of peace and serenity…maybe on the first couple of days, have a soothing bath with candles, listen to calming music with a cup of tea, or spend time with a pet…whatever is positive for *you*. After completing the 3 days of the emotional creator activity, please reflect on the following:

What emotions are difficult for you to generate (create)? What positive emotions would you like to focus on more frequently or more intentionally?

U. Compassion-Based Insight Activity

- Created by Sara Spowart, Ph.D., LMFT

One of the most important parts of happiness is understanding and applying compassion. Compassion here means the practical application of love with an understanding of situations, people, or events. Compassion can help us make sense of pain, as well as be more loving and kinder in our judgment and expectations of ourselves or others. It can bring ease and comfort to any circumstance, and greater love, insight, and detachment. The more that compassion is practiced, the easier and more natural it becomes. Through cultivating awareness of your compassion levels, it can help reduce suffering and pain, and increase happiness and well-being.

Below is the Compassion-Based Resiliency Chart. Please refer to this, as well as the reflection questions provided below.

Compassion-Based Resiliency Chart

Full, Unconditional Compassion to Self and Others
Full Compassion to Self and Others
Partial Compassion to Self and Others
Neutral on Compassion to Self and Others
Partial Negative Judgement of Self and Others
Full Negative Judgement of Self and Others
Don't Understand or Know What This Means
Unconscious Reactions, Habits and Patterns

Reflection and Discussion Questions:

a. What does *compassion* mean for you?

b. What does *compassion for others* mean?

c. When are some moments you have experienced some level of compassion? What did it feel like?

d. What is an area of your life in which you can apply greater levels of compassion to yourself or others currently? How can you apply this compassion?

e. What is something that has happened in the past where you can apply greater levels of compassion for yourself or others? How can you apply this compassion?

f. Please refer to the Compassion-Based Resiliency chart below. Where in the chart do you feel you are today?

g. Please identify where in the Compassion-Based Resiliency chart you are each day.

V. Transformation Activity
- Created by Sara Spowart, Ph.D., LMFT

> *"Energy cannot be created or destroyed; it can only be changed from one form to another."* -**Albert Einstein**

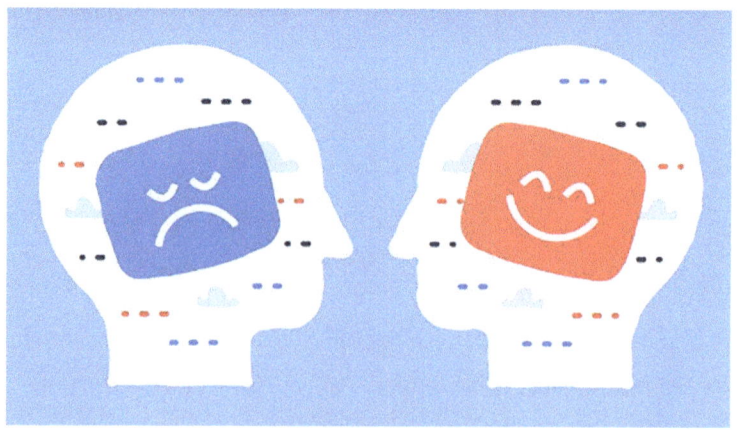

Transformation Activity

The ability and practice of transforming negative, painful emotions and suffering into positive, neutral, or uplifting emotions is a practice that can improve through awareness, repetition, detachment, and the intentional desire for change. Painful emotions tend to be more 'sticky' and 'heavy,' and like a spider web, we can get caught in them. However, if we ignore painful emotions, suppress them, or deny them… it will not make them ultimately go away. There is a balance to validating, acknowledging, and honoring pain you have and are currently experiencing…and then after it has been validated, letting it go or using it as fuel for change and creating something positive from that strong energy.

In this practice, please apply the following three prompts to something that is causing you pain, suffering, or negative emotion and has been difficult to recover from.

Practice Session 1: Please reflect on the term "radical acceptance." What does this mean to you? What are some things you have already been able to accept that were difficult in your life?

Practice Session 2: Please write or record an audio note on a negative emotion you have been struggling with, such as guilt, anxiety, depression, stress, or shame. Please consider thanking it for what it has done in your life, the negative and positive things it has brought you, and telling it kindly that you no longer need it, are ready to let it go, and live in greater harmony and acceptance of it.

Practice Session 3: Please reflect on 3 things in your life that have upset you, or you felt were harmful from your past. Below, please write each one out and reflect on the positive or potential positive that can come from each 'bad' thing. Lastly, please consider thanking each 'bad' thing for the role it has served in your life and any positive that has come or could come from it.

W. Happiness Challenge
- Created by Sara Spowart, Ph.D., LMFT

Many people have likely heard the idea that "happiness is a choice." Although there is truth to this, it is also more complicated than this. If you have experienced trauma, severe and chronic stress, mental illness, or other challenges…it becomes less easy. However, happiness can be an intention that you make for yourself every day and one that you work towards no matter what. Negativity, self-centeredness, and self-pity can be a bit like junk food for temporary self-esteem and a feeling of temporary/limited positivity. However, it is not sustainable.

Intentionally focusing on happiness every day, creates a habit and commitment to create this in your daily life. However, part of intentional happiness is detachment, mindfulness, and taking responsibility for how you feel and want to experience the world. The Happiness Challenge is an activity to help cultivate this intention and practically apply it in your daily life. It is 7 days of practicing happiness consciously and intentionally.

7 Days of Happiness Challenge

Day 1: What does it mean to you to be happy? How committed do you feel to being happy?

Day 2: What does it mean to you to be unhappy? How committed do you feel to being unhappy?

Day 3: How responsible do you feel for your happiness? What role do other people, places, and situations play in your happiness?

Day 4: Is it self-loving and kind to yourself to be happy? Is it self-loving and kind to yourself to be unhappy? What are the benefits and negatives of both?

Day 5: What role does the decision to be happy or unhappy play in someone's well-being? Is it possible to decide to be happy, no matter what, and stick to this? Or is this unrealistic and unnecessarily optimistic?

Day 6: What are some benefits that one might perceive they are gaining from feeling angry, upset, and unhappy?

Day 7: How can I take better care of myself? How can I show myself more love and compassion every day?

X. Simplification
- Created by Sara Spowart, Ph.D., LMFT

Simplification is one of the most powerful ways to improve your happiness and well-being. Fasting is one 'simplification' approach. It essentially means we look at what we can reduce or cut down in our daily lives. This can mean we 'fast' from spending one day a week, or 'fast' from negative news or negative thoughts, or fast from a certain type of food like sugar for 1 day a week. The most powerful type of fasting is one that is most applicable to you and your specific life situation. It is about rebalancing your life for the better, and realizing what is out of balance.

So, when you take a step back and reflect, what is out of balance in your life?

What could you cut down that would improve your life, and have a positive ripple effect on others?

7 Days of Simplification

Find one thing or thought you can cut down on that would help simplify your life more.

What can you 'fast' from? Can you cut down/eliminate food, spending, excess activities, and negative thoughts? What can you cut down? Please journal your 'fasting/simplification' experience for each day below.

Day 1:

Day 2:

Day 3:

Day 4:

Day 5:

Day 6:

Day 7:

Y. Intuitive Walks: The Practice of Listening to Yourself

"Aimlessness"
-Thich Nhat Hanh

A significant part of happiness is learning how to better listen to yourself and what you need. One of the greatest issues in well-being arguably, is people living lives they don't want to be living. Or rather that they don't even know who they are, or what they want. The more abuse and trauma you've experienced, oftentimes the harder it is to know what you want, how you feel, and who you are. The practice of intuitive walks can be powerful for addressing this.

With intuitive walks, you are taking time out of your day for 5-30 minutes (depending on what you prefer) and just walking anywhere. You are walking with no intention of an outcome, or goal, to achieve anything other than listening to yourself aimlessly. This practice partially comes from time spent at a Buddhist monastery by the author and personalized teaching from the head monks that was given to her. The teaching was only one word, and that was "aimlessness." Our clinging to what we think will bring pleasure, our pushing away of perceived pain...leads to a life of stress and uncertainty. By practicing aimlessness through intuitive walks, you can increase your ability to listen to your inner voice, with peace for the direction you go in, and no attachment to the result. It is a practice to increase inner peace, happiness, and inner trust in yourself.

7 Days of Inner Knowing

Participate in one 5-30 minute Intuitive Walk a day. There is no goal for this walk except to go, non-judgmentally, in whatever direction you feel you should go, and to have no intention except to listen to yourself and where the walk takes you.

Please journal on the experience for each day below.

Day 1:

Day 2:

Day 3:

Day 4:

Day 5:

Day 6:

Day 7:

Z. The Nervous System, Safety & Rest Exercise

"Rest is not a waste of time. It's a necessity."

An essential component of well-being is being able to rest. If you are always on alert and your nervous system is on the high drive and high-functioning, you will fry your adrenals, cortisol levels, and overall stress response. This is a good way to create mental illness, physical illness, and decreased stress management and resiliency response. Intentional rest is necessary, and not a waste of time. However, when you are resting, it is important to be intentional and practice presence. When you rest, you fully rest with the only goal being how well you rested.

The Nervous System, Safety & Rest Exercise is meant to help support this need for the body and nervous system to have breaks. These breaks allow us to restore ourselves so we can handle new stressors, or chronic stressors as they arise. Please practice the Nervous System, Safety, and Rest meditation below, or listen to its recording provided in this program under the meditations.

The Nervous System, Safety & Rest Meditation

Close your eyes and sit in a comfortable position, and maybe with your feet on the floor
Take a deep breath in through your nose and out through your mouth
Take another deep breath in through your nose and out through your mouth
Take one more deep breath in through your nose and out through your mouth

And as I count down from 5 to 1, feeling more and more relaxed, calm and at peace
5 to 4 feeling more relaxed
4 to 3
3 to 2 calmer and calmer
2 to 1 feeling calm, relaxed and at peace

Imagine that you are sitting near a grassy green field and peaceful forest
Breath in peace and calm
Breath out the feeling of support and safety
Notice the breath in and out and the flow of the air

Now, imagine you are standing up and then are walking towards the forest
As you walk towards the forest, you feel more and more supported, calm and at peace
Deep breath in and out, allowing yourself in this moment to be safe and supported
Breathing in support and compassion
Breathing out support and compassion

Then imagine that you are wearing a back-pack full of rocks, and these rocks are everything and anything that is weighing you down, causing you trauma, stress, pain and fear
You walk over to a lake in the forest, and this lake dissolves any and all the rocks in your backpack

One by one throwing these rocks into the lake, and they melt and dissolve away
3
2
And 1
These rocks melt and dissolve away completely
And throwing your backpack into the lake now, and it dissolves away completely
And you feel lighter and lighter, more and more at peace and at ease
Deep breath in and out,
Imagining yourself sitting in this forest by the lake
And you are filled with rest

Your head, neck and shoulders…in this moment, you feel kindness and compassion foryourself
Your arms and hands ….in this moment, your arms and hands are filled with compassion and self-kindness
Your torso, heart, chest, and stomach…kindness and compassion
Your back, hips, legs and feet…all filled with kindness and compassion

And you breathe in a feeling of compassion, and breath out
Knowing that in this moment, you are filled with compassion, love and feel at peace…

AA. Positive and Negative Projection: Know Your Own Perspective

A very powerful part of our happiness and well-being is the concept of projection. Projection may be a confusing topic and mechanism to understand our patterns and modes of operating in the world.

Projection can be described a bit like a snow globe analogy or a kaleidoscope perspective. For example, with 'negative projection', imagine you are experiencing a certain perspective where it feels very strongly that others are lying, manipulating, narcissistic, etc. Well, this is kind of like if you lived inside a snow globe for a moment and it got shaken up. Your perspective looking through the snow globe will be blocked and obstructed by the fake snow, you can't see clearly. Less often but just as powerful and deceptive, is the concept of positive projection where your perspective is just as obstructed and unclear. With positive projection, you may feel you are experiencing most people as being kinder, more loving, more caring, empathetic, harder-working, etc. than they actually are.

With both positive and negative projection we may be expressing beliefs, thoughts, feelings, perspectives that represent us and are part of us onto others. For example, a very hopeful, loyal, hard-working person may project those qualities on to others when they do not have those qualities. They may think there are many more loyal, hard-working people that you can trust and have hope in than actually exist. They are projecting their own view of the world outward and don't even realize it. This may be because the 'projector' person has those qualities themselves or they hold certain beliefs about the world that they apply outward. By contrast with negative projection, it can be that the person has experienced significant trauma and are unclearly viewing others or their negative patterns or behaviors in themselves, so strongly color their outlook that they perceive those things in others too. For example, if someone lies, cheats, steals, or are primarily 'out for themselves,' they may perceive others as doing the same thing too. It becomes the obstruction that blocks them for seeing the world clearly.

Another analogy is to look from the perspective of the kaleido-scope and understand that your perspective is colored and obstructed, if it's a beautiful or negative looking obstruction, it's still an obstruction. When we can start to notice the obstruction more and more, we can open ourselves up to greater levels of truth, clarity and insight. This is very powerful for happiness, when we start to see more clearly the stories we tell ourselves.

BB. Sentence Completion: What is it really?

A key importance in happiness is breaking 'vague' or general concepts into much more concrete, specific understandings. This is helpful for insight and understanding, for breaking patterns and attachments, and for shifting into new perspectives, and new points of view. Two exercises that can be done for 'sentence completion' are provided below and are very important for trying to break free of obstructions to your level of happiness. One exercise for 'positive sentence completion' is to take something you would like to do to increase and improve well-being and then write out or verbalize a minimum of **eight 'fill in the blanks.'** For example, if you want to do 30 minutes more walking a day, one way to increase your motivation and break through barriers on walking is sentence completion.

Walking 30 minutes more a day...

1. *helps me feel more energized every day*
2. *decreases my stress levels*
3. *helps me get into a more positive mindset*
4. *improves my physical health*
5. *improves my mental health*
6. *helps me have a better perspective on life challenges*
7. *gives me an opportunity to practice more mindfulness every day*
8. *gives my nervous system a break and a chance to calm down*

The above sentence completion breakdown demonstrates how sentence completion can be used to motivate, inspire and help improve levels of well-being and commitment to positive change. Another form of sentence completion is the reduction and breakdown of a negative thought, experience or perception as a way to loosen the grip that it might have on a person. For example, below is an example of a sentence completion exercise to help breakdown and loosen the heaviness or influence of a negative experience or emotion.

Anger...

1. *is an issue I struggle with everyday*
2. *is trying to help protect me*
3. *is hard on my body and mind and causes me stress*
4. *anger is something that is always there for me*
5. *is something that I don't need anymore everyday and it is too destructive to practice regularly*
6. *is something I learned from others and have practiced*
7. *comes out with yelling, screaming and rage for me*
8. *hurts my ability to see what is objectively and clearly true and accurate*

The above example helps to demonstrate the exploration and breakdown in understanding about a destructive emotion can help to disempower that emotion and also let it go. By investigating the destructive emotion in a non-judgmental, neutral way, it helps to improve it. This is because what we measure, you often improve.

CC.   Incredible Future Exercises

Day 1: Remembering the Positive Past (PP). Begin by spending 20 minutes or longer reflecting on positive experiences related to the goal that you would like to achieve. Write about actual successes you had in the past related to the goal or in similar areas to the goal.

For example, if your goal has to do with work, write about work-related accomplishments. If your goal concerns a relationship, write about exceptionally good times you've had in the context of your relationship. Write about your best, happiest, most memorable experiences within the domain of your goal.

Day 2: Imagining a Happy Future. For 20 minutes or longer, write about your ideal future state in the domain of your choice. Imagine that everything has gone as well as it possibly could have gone, and you attained all the goals you set for yourself.

Day 3: Creating Concrete Goals. Spend 20 minutes or so making a list of goals related to the domain of your choice.

1.   **Long-term goals.** Begin with goals that you would like achieve within a minimum of a year from now and up to 30 years from now. These should be self-resonating goals, aligned with your purpose.

2. **Medium-term goals.** Based on the long-term goals, make a list of goals for the next year. These should be challenging goals and at the same time realistic.

3. **Short-term goals.** Write down what you plan to do tomorrow, next week, and for the next month in order to achieve your medium- and ultimately long-term goals. Can you think of any habits or practices that you can introduce into your life for your goals?

Day 4: Realizing with Authentic Action

For 20 minutes or longer reflect on and write about the strengths that you plan to bring into the mix (reflecting what you're good at and what you're passionate about).   .

What values are important for you to adhere to as you realize your goals?

DD.   Positive Emotion File

You can make a positive emotion portfolio that helps support and improve positive emotions through putting together items that foster and nurture positive sentiments. For examples, you can organize an online folder that includes things like quotes, poems, artwork, music, video, audio, pictures, or anything you can think of that is expressive of the positive emotion you want to increase.

For example, if you want to increase the emotion of love, you can include quotes, images, mantras, audio, video, etc. that make you feel and think about love. Then refer back to your positive emotion folder or items every day for 5-10 minutes. You can continue to add to it, or continue to review the same items every day to further anchor and nurture the same positive emotions.

Week 1: Trapped in Patterns and Loops

We have tens of thousands of thoughts a day; it's estimated that 85-90% of them are unconscious, and about 90-95% are the same or very similar as the day before. This means that in many ways, we are on autopilot, on repeat... and without awareness, we tend to stay on 'repeat' like a software program full of repetitive codes.

Our automatic pilot patterns and stories can cause us pleasure or pain, and attachment to the stories (both positive and negative narratives) can also cause challenges. Being trapped in a cycle of the familiar, stuck in a loop of thoughts, beliefs, and feelings, creates attachment and can keep us engaged in desiring toxic lifestyles. However, the simple act of bringing awareness and identifying these patterns, loops, habits, and unconscious thought structures helps interrupt these cycles.

Why does this matter? This matters because a majority of people spend most of their waking consciousness existing in what I refer to as the 'red zone' of emotions, signifying a space of destructive emotions. Destructive emotions include shame, apathy, helplessness, blame, fear, resentment, anger, rage, guilt, sadness, depression, etc. They are emotions that hurt relationships, ourselves, and our societies. They are also emotions that tend to be re-enforcing. This implies that fear tends to bring more fear and creates a mental pattern of living by fear. Anger tends to create more anger, and you can get trapped in a painful cycle of feeling angry, which creates more anger and challenges with managing or decreasing anger.

There are different ways of identifying patterns and modes of being. A skilled therapist can be very helpful, but instead of that, mindfulness, journaling through writing or audio recordings, and practices such as yoga can be helpful. Other methods that can provide insight include creating a timeline of your life experiences and looking for patterns. Another method is to look at the chart provided below and track feelings regularly, multiple times a day, to create and bring awareness to what you are experiencing. The simple identification of feelings, thoughts, habits, and patterns is needed in this step. You are allowing yourself an opportunity to see more clearly. By noting your emotions on the chart and what 'zone' you tend to be in, you are also becoming the 'observer' of something instead of the thing itself or the reaction itself. The more we can focus on the fact that we are not the emotions, habits, patterns, and feelings - we are a separate consciousness - the more evidently, we can see the trends we have been stuck in over time.

To Complete This Week:

1. *7 Days of Compassion-Based Insight:* To become free of patterns, habits, and the things blocking our happiness, we must first see and understand what is blocking us and getting in our way. The first step to increasing happiness is achieving self-awareness and the practice of mindfulness concerning what appears to be normal or our habitual patterns. Please complete the reflections below for each day, starting with Day 1.

2. *Self-Reflections:*

   a. What was the best part of your day today? Why?

   b. What zone (red, green, blue or purple zones) do you tend to be in each day?

   c. Where on the *Trapped Cycle* are you today (#1-6)?

3. *Meditations:* Listen to one of the available meditations at least twice this week.

4. *Group/Individual Meetings:*

   a. Participate in the 30-minute live Zoom *Introduction Meeting* on the 1st day of theprogram.

   b. Participate in the 2nd live Zoom meeting as scheduled this week.

Resources for This Week:

A. Emotion Chart:

PURPLE ZONE: FREEDOM EMOTIONS

Unity, Big Picture Perspective, Integration, Freedom From 'Self', Seeing 'Self' in 'Other'

Compassion-Based Giving, Balance between 'Self' and 'Other,' Authenticity, Service, Creativity, Imagination, Faith, Inter-Dependence, Vision, Empowerment

Purpose, Meaning, Mission, Flow State, Connection, Truth, Beauty, Goals, Wisdom

BLUE ZONE: UPLIFTING & LIGHTENING EMOTIONS

Bliss, Serenity, Peace, Harmony, Self-Awareness, Balance
Joy, Enthusiasm, Abundance, Exhilaration, Hope

Compassion, Empathy, Inspiration, Clarity, Presence
Love, Appreciation, Gratitude, Devotion, Generosity

GREEN ZONE: RELIEF EMOTIONS

Cooperation, Trust, Letting Go, Detachment
Satisfaction, Amusement, Curiosity

Power, Strength, Agency, Discovery, Challenge, Discipline
Self-Esteem, Dignity, Duty, Obligation
Neutral, Acceptance, Contentment, Safety
Happy, Excited, Surprised, Fun

RED ZONE: DESTRUCTIVE & CYCLICAL EMOTIONS

Anxiety, Nervousness, Shock, Confusion, Control, Stressed, Co-Dependent
Anger, Rage, Avoidance
Guilt, Resentment
Fear, Hatred, Blame, Denial, Self-Centeredness
Sadness, Grief, Loss

Isolated, Disconnected, Lonely, Duality
Hopelessness, Resignation, Depression
Powerlessness, Overwhelm, Frozen, Terror, Trauma
Shame, Apathy, Helplessness

B. Trapped Cycles
- *Created by Sara Spowart, Ph.D., LMFT*

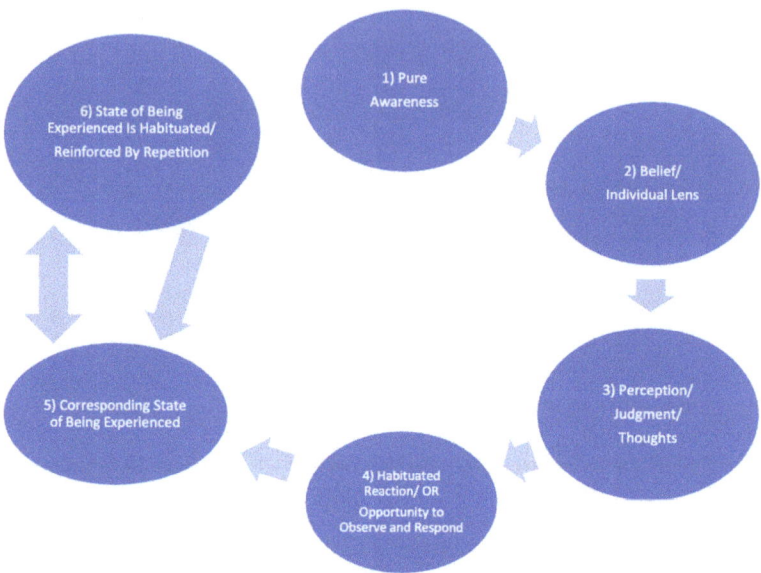

C. 21 Happiness-Based Mindfulness Hypnotherapy Meditations
- *Created by Sara Spowart, Ph.D., LMFT*

- Please select from the **21 Happiness-Based Mindfulness Hypnotherapy Meditations** on pages 6-8.

Daily Activity Each Day for 7 Days:

1. Identify *at least one moment* you experienced in the blue zone (of the emotion chart) each day this week.

Which emotion in the blue zone did you experience in this/these moment/s?

Day 1:

Day 2:

Day 3:

Day 4:

Day 5:

Day 6:

Day 7:

2. **Identify where you mostly were in terms of thoughts and emotions in the *Trapped Cycle Diagram* each day (#1-6).**

Day 1:

Day 2:

Day 3:

Day 4:

Day 5:

Day 6:

Day 7:

3. What was the best part of your day each day? Why?

Day 1:

Day 2:

Day 3:

Day 4:

Day 5:

Day 6:

Day 7:

4. Insights and Daily Reflections: *7 Days of Compassion-Based Insight.*

Please write or record an audio note to answer each question.

Day 1: What is your narrative about yourself and your life? Have you seen yourself as a happy person, a struggling, stuck, depressed, anxious, unloved, poor, rich, beautiful, ugly, etc. person?

Day 2: How was your life this time last year? How were your thoughts, feelings, story, perception of your life, and your situation? Were they similar or different?

Day 3: How was your life this time 5 years ago? How were your thoughts, feelings, story, and perception of your life and your situation? Were they similar or different?

Day 4: How do you think your life will be, 1 year from now? How might your thoughts, feelings, story, perception of your life, and your situation be similar or different?

Day 5: If there's anything you've ever felt trapped in, what would it be? What feels impossible to become free of? Please write or record an audio note for each question.

Day 6: If you were in the 'blue zone' more often, what loops or patterns from the 'red zone' would be easier to manage when they get triggered?

Please write or record an audio note for each question.

Day 7: What triggers accidentally get you into the 'red zone' on the emotion chart? What helps you get into the 'blue zone'?

Week 2: Your Identity Structure

Understanding your perception of yourself is another important aspect of creating awareness and stopping attachment, engagement, and participation in harmful cycles. Some reflection questions to consider on this...

Who do you see yourself as? Who do others perceive you as?
What words would you use to describe yourself, both 'positive' and 'negative'?

A big part of unhappiness is not knowing who we are and trying to be someone we are not or living a life that does not authentically suit us. This can easily cause situations where you may feel trapped in patterns, programs, and attachments for trying to be who you think you are 'supposed to be' and having no idea who you truly are. If you don't realize this is happening and learn to listen to your authentic self... an experience of hopelessness, depression, feelings of confusion, powerlessness, and even anger can occur. This week's materials are meant to be an introduction to better your understanding of who you are and who you are not. It is meant to encourage you to learn to listen to yourself and what best fits *your* life.

To Complete This Week:

1. *7 Days of Identity Insight:* Complete the reflections below for each day, starting with Day 1.

2. *Self-Reflections:*

   a. What zone (red, green, blue or purple) do you tend to be in each day?

   b. Where on the *Identity Layers Chart* are you today? "*What layer are you most affected by?*"

   c. Where on the *Trapped Cycle* are you today (#'s 1-6)?

3. *Meditations:* Listen to 1-2 of the hypnotherapy meditations 2 times or more this week.

4. *Group/Individual Meetings:* Participate in the 3rd live Zoom or phone meeting this week

Resources for This Week:

A. Emotion Chart:

PURPLE ZONE: FREEDOM EMOTIONS

Unity, Big Picture Perspective, Integration, Freedom From 'Self', Seeing 'Self' in 'Other'

Compassion-Based Giving, Balance between 'Self' and 'Other,' Authenticity, Service, Creativity, Imagination, Faith, Inter-Dependence, Vision, Empowerment

Purpose, Meaning, Mission, Flow State, Connection, Truth, Beauty, Goals, Wisdom

BLUE ZONE: UPLIFTING & LIGHTENING EMOTIONS

Bliss, Serenity, Peace, Harmony, Self-Awareness, Balance
Joy, Enthusiasm, Abundance, Exhilaration, Hope

Compassion, Empathy, Inspiration, Clarity, Presence
Love, Appreciation, Gratitude, Devotion, Generosity

GREEN ZONE: RELIEF EMOTIONS

Cooperation, Trust, Letting Go, Detachment
Satisfaction, Amusement, Curiosity

Power, Strength, Agency, Discovery, Challenge, Discipline
Self-Esteem, Dignity, Duty, Obligation
Neutral, Acceptance, Contentment, Safety
Happy, Excited, Surprised, Fun

RED ZONE: DESTRUCTIVE & CYCLICAL EMOTIONS

Anxiety, Nervousness, Shock, Confusion, Control, Stressed, Co-Dependent
Anger, Rage, Avoidance
Guilt, Resentment
Fear, Hatred, Blame, Denial, Self-Centeredness
Sadness, Grief, Loss

Isolated, Disconnected, Lonely, Duality
Hopelessness, Resignation, Depression
Powerlessness, Overwhelm, Frozen, Terror, Trauma
Shame, Apathy, Helplessness

B. Adapted Rational Emotive Behavior Therapy (REBT) Exercises:
   - Adapted and simplified by creator of HBM, Sara Spowart, LMFT

Reframing Negative Beliefs Example:

Negative Identified Belief: *There's no reason to be happy.*

What is the benefit of this negatively identified belief?
I get more attention from my family and others when I feel sad.

What is the harm of this negatively identified belief?
Feeling bad, not helping mood, or not wanting to stay sober.

3 Positive Alternatives to Identified Belief:

a. There is at least one reason to be happy.

b. Eventually, there could be a reason to be happy.

c. I am mostly just hurting myself with this belief.

C. Identity Layers Chart: Which layer are you most affected by?
- Created by Sara Spowart, Ph.D., LMFT

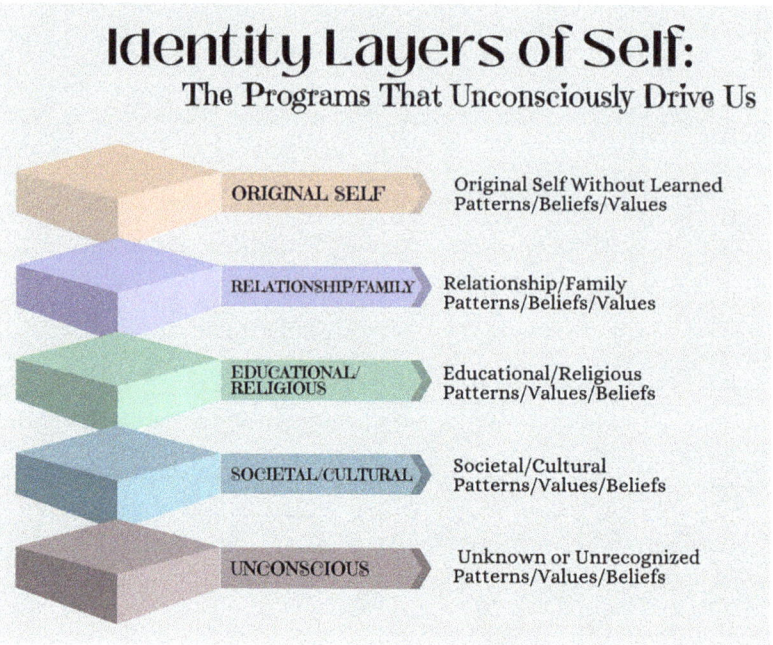

D. 21 Happiness-Based Mindfulness Hypnotherapy Meditations
- Created by Sara Spowart, Ph.D., LMFT

- Please select from the **21 Happiness-Based Mindfulness Hypnotherapy Meditations** on pages 6-8

E. Our Trapped Cycles
- Created by Sara Spowart, Ph.D., LMFT

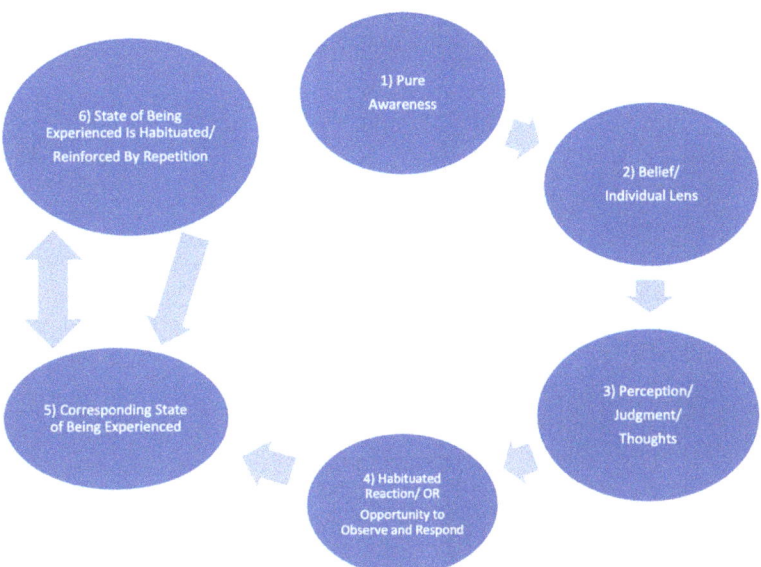

F. Adapted REBT Exercises

1. Negative Identified Belief:

What is the benefit of this negatively identified belief?

What is the harm of this negatively identified belief?

3 Positive Alternatives to Identified Belief:

a.

b.

c.

Daily Activity Each Day for 7 Days:

1. Identify where you mostly were emotionally in the chart each day (red, green, blue, or purple zones).

Which emotion in the blue zone did you experience in this/these moment/s?

Day 1:

Day 2:

Day 3:

Day 4:

Day 5:

Day 6:

Day 7:

2. Identify where on the *Identity Layers Chart* you are each day, "*What layer are you most affected by?*"

Day 1:

Day 2:

Day 3:

Day 4:

Day 5:

Day 6:

Day 7:

3. **How kind were you to yourself from 0-10? ("0" being the least, "10" being the most)**

Day 1:

Day 2:

Day 3:

Day 4:

Day 5:

Day 6:

Day 7:

4. **Insights and Daily Reflections:** *7 Days of Identity Insight.*

Day 1: What would be helpful for me to know today about myself?
Day 2: Who Am I?
Day 3: What am I afraid to admit to myself?
Day 4: Who Am I? What am I afraid to admit to myself?
Day 5: Who Am I? What am I afraid to admit to myself?
Day 6: Complete 1-2 adapted REBT exercises.
Day 7: Complete 1-2 adapted REBT exercises.

Week 3: Become a Conscious Emotion Creator

Seeing the beauty and good in everyday mindfulness – every day, take 15 minutes to notice and experience something positive in the 'blue zone.' Know that these things are 'pointers' to the experience, not the experience itself. They are a way of triggering and supporting a positive, uplifting emotion you are trying or wanting to attain. For example, seeing a beautiful tree or park may bring forward feelings of appreciation, peace, calm, and happiness. However, is it the tree and park doing this? Or is it YOU experiencing a positive reaction and interpretation? Does everyone who sees this park/nature feel these emotions, or maybe just some?

This week is to help you discover your role and the importance of your role in your happiness and well-being. Yes, of course, certain things may resonate more for certain people. However, it is still coming from you, and it is possible to learn how to increase the experience of certain emotions you want. If you don't know how to do this, another method besides finding things that help to trigger those emotions and then working to cultivate and nurture them…is to *give* the thing you want to experience. This is another way to generate the experience yourself. For example, if you wish you had felt loved as a child by your mother, maybe you can volunteer with children and be loving and nurturing towards them. This creates the energy and emotion you are looking for.

What emotions on the chart are you wanting to experience more of? How have you experienced these in the past, and what are the best ways to increase them now, even in very small ways? Our habits and patterns of relying on external things, other people, hopes, dreams, ideas…basically, everything outside of ourselves. By accepting that something inside of ourselves is disempowering and contributes to the cycles we are stuck in, we can become stronger. Instead of being a victim to certain emotions or patterns, if you could choose how you want to feel like you choose a food item on a menu...what would you want to feel?

To Complete This Week:

1. *Emotion Creator Insights* **daily exercise.**

2. *Self-Reflection:*

   a. **What zone (red, green, blue, or purple) do you tend to be in eachday?**

   b. **What was stronger each day, being in the present or being 'somewhere else'?**

3. *The 3-Day Emotion Creator* **activity.**

4. *Meditations:* **Listen to 1-2 of the hypnotherapy meditations 2x+ this week.**

5. *Group/Individual Meetings:* **Participate in the Zoom or phone meeting this week**

Resources for This Week

A. Emotion Chart

PURPLE ZONE: FREEDOM EMOTIONS

Unity, Big Picture Perspective, Integration, Freedom From 'Self', Seeing 'Self' in 'Other'

Compassion-Based Giving, Balance between 'Self' and 'Other,' Authenticity, Service, Creativity, Imagination, Faith, Inter-Dependence, Vision, Empowerment

Purpose, Meaning, Mission, Flow State, Connection, Truth, Beauty, Goals, Wisdom

BLUE ZONE: UPLIFTING & LIGHTENING EMOTIONS

Bliss, Serenity, Peace, Harmony, Self-Awareness, Balance
Joy, Enthusiasm, Abundance, Exhilaration, Hope

Compassion, Empathy, Inspiration, Clarity, Presence
Love, Appreciation, Gratitude, Devotion, Generosity

GREEN ZONE: RELIEF EMOTIONS

Cooperation, Trust, Letting Go, Detachment
Satisfaction, Amusement, Curiosity

Power, Strength, Agency, Discovery, Challenge, Discipline
Self-Esteem, Dignity, Duty, Obligation
Neutral, Acceptance, Contentment, Safety
Happy, Excited, Surprised, Fun

RED ZONE: DESTRUCTIVE & CYCLICAL EMOTIONS

Anxiety, Nervousness, Shock, Confusion, Control, Stressed, Co-Dependent
Anger, Rage, Avoidance
Guilt, Resentment
Fear, Hatred, Blame, Denial, Self-Centeredness
Sadness, Grief, Loss

Isolated, Disconnected, Lonely, Duality
Hopelessness, Resignation, Depression
Powerlessness, Overwhelm, Frozen, Terror, Trauma
Shame, Apathy, Helplessness

B. 21 Happiness-Based Mindfulness Hypnotherapy Meditations
- *Created by Sara Spowart, Ph.D., LMFT*

- Please select from the **21 Happiness-Based Mindfulness Hypnotherapy Meditations** on pages 6-8.

C. Where are you? The Present or Somewhere Else?
- *Created by Sara Spowart, Ph.D., LMFT*

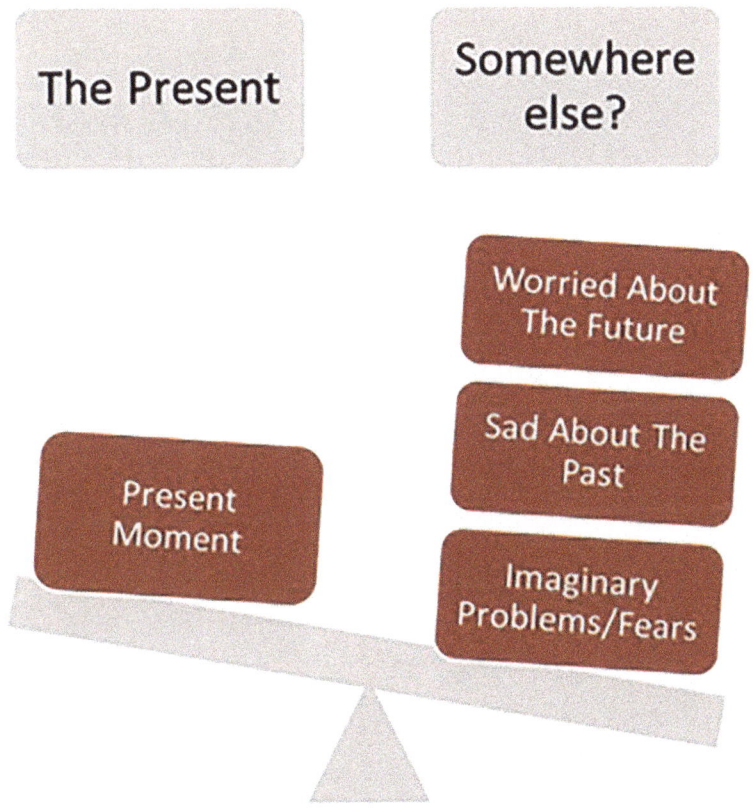

Daily Activity Each Day for 7 Days:

1. **Identify where you mostly were emotionally in the chart today (red, green, or blue zone).**

Day 1:

Day 2:

Day 3:

Day 4:

Day 5:

Day 6:

Day 7:

2. **What was stronger each day, being in the present or being 'somewhere else'?**

Day 1:

Day 2:

Day 3:

Day 4:

Day 5:

Day 6:

Day 7:

3. *Emotion Creator Insights:* **What emotions do you tend to create most? Please reflect on and identify the emotions you tend to create daily (Refer to the chart if/as needed).**

Note: Try to be as compassionate, kind, and non-judgmental towards yourself as possible. Many of us tend to get stuck in the 'red zone' on the chart, but awareness and mindfulness that it is regularly happening is a significant part of getting out of that pattern.

Day 1:

Day 2:

Day 3:

Day 4:

Day 5:

Day 6:

Day 7:

3-Day Emotion Creator Activity
Select 3 Days out of 7 Days in Week 3:

Take out at least 15 minutes each day, for 3 different days, and attempt to undergo the certain emotion you would like to experience from the chart or something similar that is either in the 'green zone' or the 'blue zone.'

You can use an object or activity to attempt to initiate these experiences for the first 2 days. On the 3rd day, try to see if you can cultivate that emotion on your own.

For example, if you choose the emotion of peace and serenity… maybe on the first couple of days, have a soothing bath with candles, listen to calming music with a cup of tea, or spend time with a pet… whatever is positive for *you.*

After completing the 3 days of 'green' and 'blue zone' creation activities, please reflect on the following:

What emotions are most difficult for you to create in the green or blue zone? Please spend at least 5 minutes writing or recording an audio note about the positive emotions that are hardest for you to experience after completing this 3-day activity.

Week 4: Turning Painful Things into Strengths

One of the traps that can happen with the 'red zone' emotions is not even realizing you are experiencing them and are stuck in repetitive patterns and reactivity within them. Weeks 1-3 were focused on creating awareness of patterns you may be stuck in, your general emotional tendencies and habits, and decided to intentionally create the emotions you would like to experience and focus more on that. In Week 4, we look at how we can shift and change painful thoughts, feelings, and experiences into something positive. Suffering happens to everyone at some point and in different forms. However, it is possible to turn trauma, pain, and 'red zone' emotions into something that benefits yourself and others when seen from different vantage points.

Turning painful things into positives is not meant to invalidate the destructive, challenging emotions and experiences you have had. Rather, it is meant to help empower you to regain control – at least partially - over your life and move forward from the experience. It is a way of redefining what has happened in your past or present so that you can see yourself and the negative emotions through a new perspective and create something constructive from it.

During This Week You Will Complete:

1. *3 Days of Transformation* to shift negative red zone emotions into green and blue zone emotions. Please complete the reflections below for each day, starting with Day 1.

2. *Self-Reflection:*

   a. Identify *at least one moment* you experienced in the blue zone (of the emotion chart) each day. *Which emotion in the blue zone did you experience in this/these moment/s?*

3. *Meditations:* Listen to 1-2 of the hypnotherapy meditations 2x+ this week.

4. *Group/Individual Meetings:* Participate in the 5th live Zoom or phone meeting this week

Resources for This Week

A. Emotion Chart

Uplifting and Lighening Emotions
Bliss, Serenity, Peace, Harmony, Self-Awareness, Balance
Joy, Enthusiasm, Abundance, Exhilaration, Hope
Compassion, Empathy, Inspiration, Clarity, Presence
Love, Appreciation, Gratitude, Devotion, Generosity

B. 21 Happiness-Based Mindfulness Hypnotherapy Meditations
- Created by Sara Spowart, Ph.D., LMFT

- Please select from the **21 Happiness-Based Mindfulness Hypnotherapy Meditations** on pages 6-8.

C. 3 Days of Transformation (Choose any 3 days out of the 7) this week to complete:

Day 1: Please reflect on the term "radical allowance." What does this mean to you? What are some things you have already been able to accept that were difficult in your life?

Day 2: Please write or record an audio note on a negative emotion you have been struggling with, such as guilt, anxiety, depression, stress, or shame. Please consider thanking it for what it has done in your life, the negative and positive things it has brought you, and telling it kindly that you no longer need it, are ready to let it go, and live in greater harmony and acceptance of it.

Day 3: Please reflect on 3 things in your life that have upset you, or you felt were harmful from your past. Below, please write each one out and reflect on the positive or potential positive that can come from each 'bad' thing. Lastly, please consider thanking each 'bad' thing for the role it has served in your life and any positive that has come or could come from it.

Daily Activity Each Day for 7 Days:

Identify *at least one moment* you experienced in the blue zone (of the emotion chart) each day this week.

Which emotion in the blue zone did you experience in this/these moment/s?

Day 1:

Day 2:

Day 3:

Day 4:

Day 5:

Day 6:

Day 7:

Week 5: Taking Responsibility for Your Happiness

One of the great challenges with happiness is the transition from being in the 'red zone' of negative emotions or feeling like a victim to feeling like we have more power and control over ourselves and can make small steps (or even big ones) towards more positive emotions and feeling like we have more agency and influence over our internal state of being. We may not always even be able to change our outer circumstances at all or very much, but we can work to internally feel better. This is a great act of self-kindness, self-love, and compassion for ourselves when we feel stuck. It is acknowledging that you love yourself enough that you want to feel better, even if it takes a while for outer circumstances to change. Often, destructive emotions like anger, anxiety, stress, guilt, shame, and hopelessness tend to create more and more of those emotional experiences. By starting from a state of betterment and focusing on increasing that, you are not invalidating your negative experiences...rather, you are declaring that you are valuable enough and deserve to feel better, no matter what has occurred.

This week, we will be learning and focusing on activities that help with increasing individual agency, empowerment, and accountability in our lived experience with happiness. This does not mean everything will bring joy externally. However, it means we can work to create an internal state of happiness and well-being, regardless of challenging outward circumstances.

During This Week You Will Complete:

1. *7-Day Happiness Challenge*: Complete the reflections below for each day, starting with Day 1.

2. *Self-Reflection*:

    a. Rate each day this week, from 0-10 ("0" being the least, "10" being the most), how committed you are to being happy every day.

3. *7 Days of Simplification*: Engage in one simplification activity each day this week. Simplification refers to small ways you can reduce stress, unnecessary busyness, addiction to activity, and discomfort with having little to do and stillness.

4. *Meditations:* Listen to 1-2 of the hypnotherapy meditations 2x+ this week.

5. *Group/Individual Meetings:* Participate in the 6th live Zoom or phone meeting this week

Resources for This Week:

A. 21 Happiness-Based Mindfulness Hypnotherapy Meditations
- Created by Sara Spowart, Ph.D., LMFT

- Please select from the **21 Happiness-Based Mindfulness Hypnotherapy Meditations** on pages 6-8.

B. 7 Days of Happiness Challenge

Day 1: What does it mean to you to be happy? How committed do you feel to being happy?

Day 2: What does it mean to you to be unhappy? How committed do you feel to being unhappy?

Day 3: How responsible do you feel for your happiness? What role do other people, places, and situations play in your happiness?

Day 4: Is it self-loving and kind to yourself to be happy? Is it self-loving and kind to yourself to be unhappy? What are the benefits and negatives of both?

Day 5: What role does the decision to be happy or unhappy play in someone's well-being? Is it possible to decide to be happy, no matter what, and stick to this? Or is this unrealistic and unnecessarily optimistic?

Day 6: What are some benefits that one might perceive they are gaining from feeling angry, upset, and unhappy?

Day 7: How can I take better care of myself? How can I show myself more love and compassion every day?

C. 7 Days of Simplification:

Find one thing or thought you can cut down on that would help simplify your life more.

What can you 'fast' from? Can you cut down/eliminate food, spending, and excess activities? What can you cut down?

Day 1:

Day 2:

Day 3:

Day 4:

Day 5:

Day 6:

Day 7:

Daily Activity For 7 Days:

Rate each day this week, from 0-10 ("0" being not at all and "10" being the most), how committed you are to being happy every day.

Please also complete the 7 Days of Happiness Challenge and the 7 Days of Simplification Activity.

Day 1:

Day 2:

Day 3:

Day 4:

Day 5:

Day 6:

Day 7:

Week 6: Living and Loving Our Life and Ourselves on Purpose

There is value in living our lives 'on purpose' or with intentionality. Creating intentions for ourselves, our families, communities, relationships, and how we want to contribute and engage with ourselves and others is important for one's happiness. Instead of living in a reactionary manner or a manner habituated by patterns and norms, it is valuable to think about being aware and deciding how you want to experience your inner world and working towards that goal. We exist in systems within ourselves, our families, communities, societies, cultures, and more. Therefore, individuals exist within systems that are connected directly and indirectly with others. An analogy could be with a fish bowl full of fish. Whatever one fish does, indirectly impacts the whole fish bowl.

Therefore, there is value in kindness towards yourself and others and in being happy, hopeful, and inspired. Not only does it help you with your own mental, emotional, physical, and relational health, but it also positively impacts those indirectly or directly associated with you. This week, the topic we will be working on will be increasing and maintaining conscious kindness and increasing your level of inspiration and motivation about your sense of purpose and your life. We will also explore ways to take the skills learned from this course and implement them in more manageable, long-term ways.

During This Week You Will Complete:

1. *7 Days of Kindness:* to help increase happiness levels and move yourself to experience the green and blue zone emotions more often.

2. *Increase Your Inspiration:* Complete the prompts below to increase insight and improve motivation and inspiration.

3. *Self-Reflection:*

    a. Blue Zone Identification Each Day

4. *Meditations:* Listen to one of the available meditations provided in the program at least thrice this week.

5. *Group/Individual Meetings:* Participate in the individual/ group meeting by Zoom or phone

Resources for This Week:

A. **21 Happiness-Based Mindfulness Hypnotherapy Meditations**
- Created by Sara Spowart, Ph.D., LMFT

  • Please select from the **21 Happiness-Based Mindfulness Hypnotherapy Meditations** on pages 6-8.

B. Blue Zone

Uplifting and Lighening Emotions
Bliss, Serenity, Peace, Harmony, Self-Awareness, Balance
Joy, Enthusiasm, Abundance, Exhilaration, Hope
Compassion, Empathy, Inspiration, Clarity, Presence
Love, Appreciation, Gratitude, Devotion, Generosity

Daily Activity Each Day for 7 Days:

1. Identify *at least one moment* you experienced in the blue zone (of the emotion chart) each day this week. *Which emotion in the blue zone did you experience in this/these moment/s and why?*

Day 1:

Day 2:

Day 3:

Day 4:

Day 5:

Day 6:

Day 7:

2. *Increase Your Inspiration:*

Day 1: What does it mean to feel inspired to you? What helps you to know you are inspired?

Day 2:

- Is there anything you'd like to do or experience in your life that you haven't done yet that could be positive and life-affirming for you?
- Please read these phrases and select one (or create one) that feels most supportive for you.

I am committed to being happy and healthy no matter what.
I am inherently valuable no matter what.
My life is getting better and better every day in every way.
I always make small, baby steps towards a better future.
I care about myself and how I feel.
I experience positive emotions every day.

Day 3: Was there anything that made you laugh today?

Day 4: Part of happiness is not only attaining things we think we want or need; it may also be the experience of positive emotions and relief from negative emotions that can exist as an internal state, regardless of current life circumstances. What does this mean to you?

Day 5: How worthwhile is it to focus on increasing happiness in your life? Why might it make a difference?

Day 6: How has your perception of happiness changed during this program?

Day 7: What do you feel has changed about yourself, if anything, throughout this course?

3. *7 Days of Kindness:*

For days 2-7, please intentionally do one act of kindness for yourself or someone else today.

Day 1: For Day 1 Only…

- Think of a cause or situation you care about that is happening in your community, country, or the world.
- Please read these phrases and select one (or create one) that feels most supportive for you. *I always make choices to help increase my happiness; I love myself unconditionally; I care about myself and how I feel; I feel compassion for others.*

Day 1:

Day 2:

Day 3:

Day 4:

Day 5:

Day 6:

Day 7:

Week 7: The Joy of Service and Authenticity

An essential part of happiness and well-being is to be of service and function from a sense of purpose. It may not be a popular notion, but selfishness and self-centeredness are not the path to happiness and freedom. Selfishness or self-centeredness is a good method to create unhappiness, stress, and an unnecessary focus on your own perceived concerns and patterns. Authentic service, done without the desire for attention or recognition, is one of the most powerful ways to improve happiness. Living in a state of authentic service towards others means that you are moving beyond yourself and working towards something positive. It is also a form of practical love in action. It is a way to get out of the red zone, build self-esteem and confidence, and break up trapped patterns and identity structures. Authentic service benefits your happiness as much as others, and finding your mode and passion for positive authentic service can help inspire greater happiness in this domain of well-being.

During This Week You Will Complete:

1. *7 Days of Kindness:* to help increase happiness levels and move yourself to experience the green and blue zone emotions more often.

2. *Self Reflection:*

   a. *How much were you living in authentic service today from 0-10?*

3. *Meditations:* Listen to one of the available meditations provided in the program at least thrice this week.

4. *Group/Individual Meetings:* Participate in the individual/group meeting by Zoom or phone

Resources for This Week:

A. *7 Days of Kindness:*

For days 2-7 please intentionally do one act of kindness for yourself or someone else today.

Day 1: For Day 1 Only…

- Think of a cause or situation you care about that is happening in your community, country, or the world.
- Please read these phrases and select one (or create one) that feels most supportive for you. *I always make choices to help increase my happiness; I love myself unconditionally; I care about myself and how I feel; I feel compassion for others.*

Day 1:

Day 2:

Day 3:

Day 4:

Day 5:

Day 6:

Day 7:

B. Service
- Created by Sara Spowart, Ph.D., LMFT

How *much are you in authentic service* today from 0-10? ("0" being not at all and "10" being the most)

Daily Activity Each Day for 7 Days:

1. **Identify how much you were in a state of *authentic service* today from 0-10. ("0" being not at all and "10" being the most)**

Day 1:

Day 2:

Day 3:

Day 4:

Day 5:

Day 6:

Day 7:

2. *7 Days of Kindness:*

Please intentionally do one act of kindness for *yourself* or *someone else* today.

Day 1: For Day 1 Only...

- Think of a cause or situation you care about that is happening in your community, country, or the world.

- Please read these phrases and select one (or create one) that feels most supportive for you. *I always make choices to help increase my happiness; I love myself unconditionally; I care about myself and how I feel; I feel compassion for others.*

Day 1:

Day 2:

Day 3:

Day 4:

Day 5:

Day 6:

Day 7:

Week 8: Love

A major component of well-being is love. Love can refer to kindness to others, kindness to yourself, friendship love, familial love, romantic love, love for humanity, and more. It can adapt and take so many forms and applications. So how do we put this into practice? How do we put this into action? In this week and next, we will cover tangible exercises to improve and better understand the experience of love in your life. Love is a huge transformer of negative emotions and circumstances into positive, uplifting experiences. Love opens and connects, while fear tends to shut down and close off. Some practices that help us to increase our experience of love, peace, and contentment include the gratitude manifestation and fear exercise, as well as the self-love and other-love awareness exercises.

What does love mean to you? Do you feel it's referring to only romantic, friendship, or familial love? What if it's a larger, encompassing life force energy that makes up and manifests all that exists? What if by focusing on love, you are opening yourself up to feeling happier than you've ever been before?

During This Week You Will Complete:

1. *Body Love Exercise*

2. *Gratitude/Manifestation and Fear*

3. *Self-Love and Other-Love*

4. *Meditations:* **Listen to one of the available meditations provided in the program at least thrice this week.**

5. *Group/Individual Meetings:* Participate in the individual/ group meeting by Zoom or phone.

Resources for This Week:

A. Body Love Exercise
- Created by Sara Spowart, Ph.D., LMFT

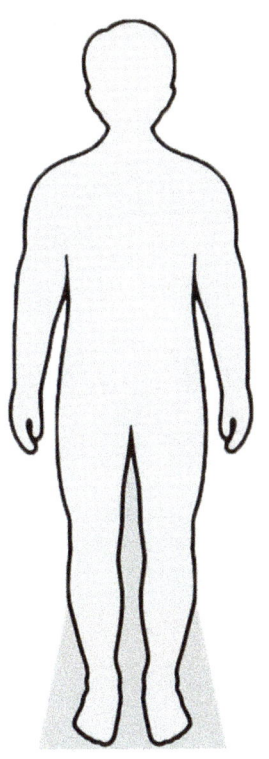

Love/Like/Neutral/ Don't Like/Hate…
Face & Parts of Face:
Upper Body Area:
Belly and Torso:
Hips, Legs and Lower Body:
Other Body Parts of Concern:

B. Gratitude/Manifestation and Fear Exercise

1. **Today what are you feeling thankful for? (both in manifested and yet-to-be-manifested form)**

2. Today what are you having fear about?

Example:

Gratitude/Manifested Gratitude: I am so happy and thankful today because I got a grant for $50 million to help bring greater happiness, kindness, and love into the world! I am so happy and thankful because I bought a house today!

My Fears: I am afraid I will never have a healthy body or get strong and in shape. I'm afraid I won't be able to pay all my bills on time.

C. Self-Love and Other Love: Love and Awareness Charts
  - *Created by Sara Spowart, Ph.D., LMFT*

Self-Love Chart

Love Myself Unconditionally
Love Myself
Like Myself
Neutral about Myself
Don't Like Myself
Hate Myself
Don't Understand or Know What This Means
Unconscious Reactions, Habits, and Patterns

Other-Love Chart

Love Others Unconditionally
Love Others
Like Others
Neutral about Others
Don't Like Others
Hate Others
Don't Understand or Know What This Means
Unconscious Reactions, Habits, and Patterns

D. Mirror of Self Exercise

- Created by Sara Spowart, Ph.D., LMFT

Authentic Living*

Healthy Narcissism*

Living By 'Shoulds'

Playing Roles

Wearing a Mask

Unhealthy Narcissism

Daily Activity Each Day for 7 Days:

1. Identify *how you felt about your body* each day this week. Please refer to the Body Love Image.

Day 1:

Day 2:

Day 3:

Day 4:

Day 5:

Day 6:

Day 7:

2. Mirror of Self. Identify where you were on the Mirror of Self-activity each day.

Day 1:

Day 2:

Day 3:

Day 4:

Day 5:

Day 6:

Day 7:

3. **Please identify where you are in the Self-Love/Other-Love Charts each day.**

Day 1:

Day 2:

Day 3:

Day 4:

Day 5:

Day 6:

Day 7:

Week 9: Love (Continued...)

This week we continue to explore the themes from Week 8 regarding the significance of love in improving levels of happiness and wellbeing. During this week you will complete the Self-Love and Other-Love Activity, the Mirror of Self-activity, the Hope Spectrum Activity, as well as the meditations and weekly meeting. All of these are intended to further cultivate the creation of greater levels of love in your life, as well as radical acceptance and awareness of current circumstances. Through awareness and honest observation alone, this can create a shift toward a more positive direction and slow down the momentum of old patterns, habits, and harmful perspectives.

During This Week You Will Complete:

1. *Self-Love and Other-Love Activity*

2. **Mirror of Self Activity**

3. *Hope Spectrum Activity*

4. *Meditations:* **Listen to one of the available meditations provided in the program at least thrice this week.**

5. *Group/Individual Meetings:* **Participate in the individual/ group meeting by Zoom or phone**

Resources for This Week:

A. Self-Love and Other Love: Love and Awareness Charts
- Created by Sara Spowart, Ph.D., LMFT

Self-Love Chart

Love Myself Unconditionally
Love Myself
Like Myself
Neutral about Myself
Don't Like Myself
Hate Myself
Don't Understand or Know What This Means
Unconscious Reactions, Habits, and Patterns

Other-Love Chart

Love Others Unconditionally
Love Others
Like Others
Neutral about Others
Don't Like Others
Hate Others
Don't Understand or Know What This Means
Unconscious Reactions, Habits, and Patterns

B. Mirror of Self
- Created by Sara Spowart, Ph.D., LMFT

C. Hope Spectrum

- Created by Sara Spowart, PhD, LMFT

Toxic Hope (Delusional Hope/Toxic Positivity)
Unhealthy Levels of Hope (Delusional positive levels of hope, and as a result stay in abusive, unhealthy, or painful situations)
Healthy Hope (Acknowledgement of reality and current situation, compassion for levels of suffering, and ability to form hopeful ideas for the future)
Unhealthy Levels of Hope (Insufficient hope levels and sadness, anxiety, and depression as a result)
Toxic Hope (Lack of Hope/Overly Negative Hopelessness)

Daily Activity Each Day for 7 Days:

1. Identify where you were on the *Self-Love and Other-Love Charts* each day.

Day 1:

Day 2:

Day 3:

Day 4:

Day 5:

Day 6:

Day 7:

2. Mirror of Self. Identify where you were on the Mirror of Self-activity each day.

Day 1:

Day 2:

Day 3:

Day 4:

Day 5:

Day 6:

Day 7:

3. **Hope Spectrum. Identify where you were on the *Hope Spectrum* activity each day regarding a challenging situation you are dealing with.**

Day 1:

Day 2:

Day 3:

Day 4:

Day 5:

Day 6:

Day 7:

Week 10: Taking a Bigger Picture

A major component of happiness is the ability to see beyond our limited perspective. Our limited perspective will inevitably cause pain and suffering regardless of how great our lives are. If we are stuck in our own mindset and limited viewpoint, any happiness and well-being we experience is inevitably short-term and limited. There will always be something around the corner or even in the next moment that becomes upsetting. This is partly because when we view things from only our perspective it becomes very easy to feel threatened, afraid, confused, angry, anxious, or depressed. If we see ourselves as a fragile, limited self, life is much harder. For example, if you think of a snow globe, if you take a snow globe perspective, there is a limited viewpoint inside the glass ball and snowflakes block clear vision of the glass. If we are in our little world, it is like being inside a snow globe and our perspective of the world is covered and blocked by the snow in it and it's impossible to see clearly. When we take a Bird's Eye View, we can then see much more clearly and see beyond our limited little perspective. It is liberating and can help increase empathy and compassion for others, which also increases levels of happiness and well-being.

During This Week You Will Complete:

1. *Bird's Eye View*

2. *Future Jumping*

3. *Meditations:* **Listen to one of the available meditations provided in the program at least thrice this week.**

4. *Group/Individual Meetings:* **Participate in the individual/group meeting by Zoom or phone.**

Resources for This Week:

A. Bird's Eye View
- *Created by Sara Spowart, Ph.D., LMFT*

Bird's Eye View Activity: Imagine each day the perspective of at least one other person in your life. What would it be like to experience their emotions, thoughts, and physical sensations? What would life be like through their eyes for just 1 minute today?

B. Future Jumping
- *Created by Sara Spowart, Ph.D., LMFT*

Visual for 2 minutes each day the 'future you' 1 year from now. Where are you going? How is it different from the current you? What advice would this future you have for you that you can bring into the now?

Daily Activity Each Day for 7 Days:

1. **Bird's Eye View Activity: Imagine each day the perspective of at least one other person in your life. What would it be like to experience their emotions, thoughts, and physical sensations? What would life be like through their eyes for just 1 minute today?**

Day 1:

Day 2:

Day 3:

Day 4:

Day 5:

Day 6:

Day 7:

2. **Visual for 2 minutes each day the 'future you' 1 year from now. Where are you going? How is it different from the current you? What advice would this future you have for you that you can bring into the now?**

Day 1:

Day 2:

Day 3:

Day 4:

Day 5:

Day 6:

Day 7:

Week 11: Always Feel Connected

A major part of happiness is feeling some sense of connection. One of the great issues of unhappiness is feeling a sense of disconnection and feeling alone. According to the World Health Organization, depression, isolation, and loneliness are the biggest issues in the world today for health and on the whole. We are all extremely interconnected, however it may not always feel that way. Connection is an essential part of our wellness and even physical health. However, the connection doesn't have to be with people. It can be a connection to nature, to animals, to a cause, to a purpose…something that is bigger than you. If you are trapped in your mind with your thoughts and feelings that repeat cyclically, you can feel cut off. You aren't disconnected or cut off, but you will have the experience of being and feeling cut off from a deeper connection. This feeling of disconnection can lead to toxic, harmful behaviors and severe depression, anxiety, or other mental health struggles.

Bringing awareness to the experience of connection or disconnection is powerful for beginning the process of change. If you feel alone, lonely, or cut off…awareness of this is not meant to create despair. Rather, it is to start the process of awareness for how to increase the feeling of connection and the ways and mechanisms to better achieve this. It is impossible to not be greatly interconnected with each other and everything. However, we may feel a sense of disconnection and cut-off and this emotional experience is extremely painful.

During This Week You Will Complete:

1. *Duality Exercise*

2. *Clinging or Detached*

3. *Always Feel Connected Ratings*

4. *Meditations:* Listen to one of the available meditations provided in the program at least thrice this week.

5. *Group/Individual Meetings:* Participate in the individual/group meeting by Zoom or phone.

Resources for This Week:

A. Duality
  - Created by Sara Spowart, Ph.D., LMFT

  This
  That
  This AND That

Journal in 4-7 sentences something that you are struggling with and seems to be dualistic, but maybe could be 'this' AND 'that.' What are areas of your life that have caused pain, difficulty, and stress thinking there is only 'this' or 'that' but not 'this and that?'

What is the benefit of thinking it's 'this' or 'that'?

What is the benefit of considering the thing you are struggling with has more than one 'right' answer, or more than one 'wrong' answer?

Can you abide by this ambiguity?

B. Clinging or Detached: Chart of Intention
  - Created by Sara Spowart, Ph.D., LMFT

Fully Aware of My Energy State and Living with Clear Intention
Partially Aware of My Energy State and Living Partially with Intention and Partially through Reaction and fear of loss or change
Not aware of energy state and not living with intention, living through fear of loss or change and with reaction to what is perceived as pleasurable or painful

C. Always Feel Connected Ratings

- Created by Sara Spowart, Ph.D., LMFT

Everyday rate how *connected* you feel from 0-10 ("0" is not connected and "10" is the most connected)

Daily Activity Each Day for 7 Days:

1. **Identify *how connected you feel* each day this week (from 0-10):**

Day 1:

Day 2:

Day 3:

Day 4:

Day 5:

Day 6:

Day 7:

2. **Identify where you were on the *Chart of Intention* each day this week:**

Day 1:

Day 2:

Day 3:

Day 4:

Day 5:

Day 6:

Day 7:

3. **Complete the Duality Activity at least one time this week***

Week 12: Sustainability Beyond the Program

1. Daily Zone of Self-Love

What zone are you in every day? Check-in! ☺

Love Myself Unconditionally
Love Myself
Like Myself
Neutral about Myself
Don't Like Myself
Hate Myself
Don't Understand or Know What This Means
Unconscious Reactions, Habits, and Patterns

2. **Daily Zone of Other-Love**

What zone are you in every day? Check-in! ☺

Love Others Unconditionally
Love Others
Like Others
Neutral about Others
Don't Like Others
Hate Others
Don't Understand or Know What This Means
Unconscious Reactions, Habits, and Patterns

3. **Listen to 1 hypnotherapy or do 1 self-care exercise every day for at least 10-15 minutes*****

4. **Check in with the "A-Z's of Happiness" every week and select one activity to do from them** ☺

For Instructors of Happiness-Based Mindfulness:

1. **Participate in an initial training meeting with the program's creator, Sara Spowart, Ph.D., LMFT, and review the program, core concepts, course set-up, and activities.**

2. **Please complete Happiness-Based Mindfulness over 12 sessions in total. Completing the program will help you be ready to teach so you are familiar with and have a deep understanding of the material.**

3. **Please read and reference the required materials listed below on topics that will be important for reflection and discussion from participants. These include an understanding of the concepts of radical acceptance, mindfulness for happiness, reframing negative beliefs and thoughts, mindfulness in everyday life for the improvement of emotions, and self-kindness.**

Required Reading Materials for Instructors in Training:

Provided Through Accompanying PDFs for Instructors in Training

Hook, J. N., Hodge, A. S., Zhang, H., Van Tongeren, D. R., & Davis, D. E. (2023). Minimalism,voluntary simplicity, and well-being: A systematic review of the empirical literature. *TheJournal of Positive Psychology, 18*(1), 130-141.

Honmore, V. M. (2023). Mindfulness, Happiness and Well-being among Adults. *Indian Journal of Positive Psychology, 14*(2), 184–187.

Rowland, L., & Curry, O. S. (2019). A range of kindness activities boosts happiness. *The Journal of Social Psychology, 159*(3), 340-343.

Segal. (2023). Does acceptance lead to change? Training in radical acceptance improves the implementation of cognitive reappraisal. *Behavior Research and Therapy. 164.*

Youth-Focused HBM

Created by Sara Spowart, PhD, DMFT, LMFT, MPA

Table of Contents

Resources For the Sessions:

A. Emotion Chart

Blue Zone

Love, Peace, Joy, Gratitude, Harmony, Empathy, Compassion

Green Zone

Safety, Neutral, Happy, Contentment, Challenge, Self-Esteem

Red Zone

**Anger, Fear, Anxiety, Hatred, Blame, Denial,
Sadness, Shame, Powerlessness**

Blue Zone:

Uplifting and Lighening Emotions
Bliss, Serenity, Peace, Harmony, Self-Awareness, Balance
Joy, Enthusiasm, Abundance, Exhilaration, Hope
Compassion, Empathy, Inspiration, Clarity, Presence
Love, Appreciation, Gratitude, Devotion, Generosity

B. Adapted Rational Emotive Behavior Therapy (REBT) Exercises:
- Adapted and simplified by creator of HBM, Sara Spowart, LMFT

Reframing Negative Beliefs Example:

Negative Identified Belief: *There's no reason to be happy*

What is the benefit of this negative identified belief?
I get more attention from my family and others when I feel sad

What is the harm of this negative identified belief?
Feeling bad, not helping mood or wanting to stay sober

3 Positive Alternatives to Identified Belief:

a. There is at least one reason to be happy

b. Eventually there could be a reason to be happy

c. I am mostly just hurting myself with this belief

C. Identity Layers Chart: Which layer are you most affected by?
- Made by HBM creator, Sara Spowart, PhD, LMFT

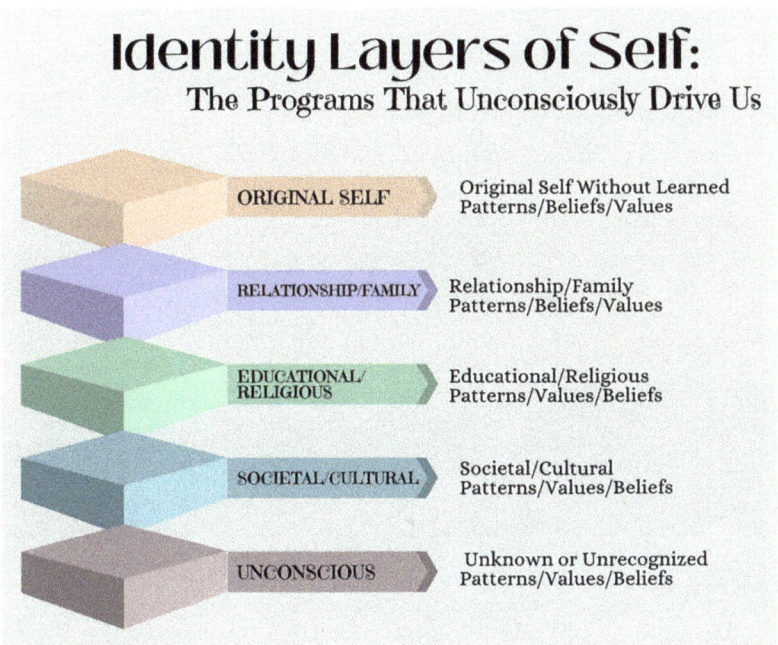

D. Adapted Rational Emotive Behavior Therapy (REBT) Exercise
- Made by HBM creator, Sara Spowart, LMFT

1) Negative Identified Belief:

What is the benefit of this negative identified belief?

What is the harm of this negative identified belief?

3 Positive Alternatives to Identified Belief:

a.

   b.

   c.

E. Compassion-Based Resiliency Chart
   - Made by HBM creator, Sara Spowart, PhD, LMFT

Full, Unconditional Compassion to Self and Others
Full Compassion to Self and Others
Partial Compassion to Self and Others
Neutral on Compassion to Self and Others
Partial Negative Judgement of Self and Others
Full Negative Judgement of Self and Others
Don't Understand or Know What This Means
Unconscious Reactions, Habits and Patterns

F. The Nervous System, Safety & Rest Exercise

Close your eyes and sit in a comfortable position, and maybe with your feet on the floor
Take a deep breath in through your nose and out through your mouth
Take another deep breath in through your nose and out through your mouth
Take one more deep breath in through your nose and out through your mouth

As I count down from 5 to 1, feeling more and more relaxed, calm, and at peace
5 to 4 feeling more relaxed
4 to 3
3 to 2 calmer and calmer
2 to 1 feeling calm, relaxed and at peace

Imagine that you are sitting near a grassy green field and a peaceful forest
Breathe in peace and calm
Breathe out the feeling of support and safety
Notice the breath in and out and the flow of the air

Now, imagine you are standing up and then walking towards the forest
As you walk toward the forest, you feel more and more supported, calm, and at peace
Deep breath in and out, allowing yourself in this moment to be safe and supported
Breathing in support and compassion
Breathing out support and compassion

Then imagine that you are wearing a backpack full of rocks, and these rocks are everything and anything that is weighing you down, causing you trauma, stress, pain, and fear
You walk over to a lake in the forest, and this lake dissolves all the rocks in your backpack
One by one throw these rocks into the lake, and they melt and dissolve away
3
2
And 1

These rocks melt and dissolve away completely
And throwing your backpack into the lake now, and it dissolves away completely
And you feel lighter and lighter, more and more at peace and ease

Deep breath in and out,
Imagining yourself sitting in this forest by the lake
And you are filled with rest

Your head, neck, and shoulders…in this moment, it is safe to rest
Your arms and hands ….in this moment, it is safe to rest
Your torso, heart, chest, and stomach…rest
Your back, hips, legs, and feet…all rest

And you breathe in a feeling of rest and breathe out
Knowing that at this moment, it is safe to rest, relax, and experience some peace…

Session 1: Emotions can be confusing: The Emotion Chart

We have many thousands of thoughts a day most of these we don't even realize we are having and most of them are similar to the day before. Like a software program on a computer, we go on repeat in a lot of ways, and on autopilot. Sometimes these patterns are helpful, but a lot of times they cause problems with how we feel and what we do every day.

But, by bringing awareness to how we feel, we can overcome these 'repeat' patterns or feelings that cause confusion or stress. We can notice how we feel and what we are stuck in by certain activities and practices like the "Emotion Chart." The Emotion Chart is a chart that helps you identify what you are feeling, how you want to feel, and why you are feeling the way you are. But it is also a tool to help create awareness and practice mindfulness of feelings. Just by noticing something, in a kind and non-judgmental way, we start to improve it and feel better. By noticing what we are feeling and what we want to feel every day in a detached way, we become more mindful and happier over time.

Here is an Emotion Chart for you to check out!

Blue Zone
Love, Peace, Joy, Gratitude, Harmony, Empathy, Compassion
Green Zone
Safety, Neutral, Happy, Contentment, Challenge, Self-Esteem
Red Zone
Anger, Fear, Anxiety, Hatred, Blame, Denial, Sadness, Shame, Powerlessness

Here is this chart you can see the destructive, and painful emotions are in the 'Red Zone.' The middle, pleasant emotions are in the 'Green Zone.' The uplifting emotions are the 'Blue Zone.' The Red Zone emotions tend to be stuck in loops and repeat over and over again. It can be really difficult to get out of them and they tend to cause really strong reactions and make it difficult to just notice, be detached and observe the feeling. The Red Zone also tends to be heavy and sticky, and it can feel that you are stuck there. The more often you have Red Zone feelings, the more they are 'watered' and grow. The more you have Blue Zone feelings, the more those increase and grow.

But why does this matter? Most people are spending a lot of their time in the Red Zone and this makes it harder to do well in school, with family, with friends, with self-esteem, relationships, performance, energy levels, sleep, etc. If we are in the Red Zone a lot, our lives are much harder and we are not as happy as we could be. Therefore, it's good to try to notice the Red Zone emotions when they are happening, and try to encourage ourselves towards the Green and Blue ☺

First Exercise:

1. *The Emotion Chart Exercise:*

Blue Zone

Love, Peace, Joy, Gratitude, Harmony, Empathy, Compassion

Green Zone

Safety, Neutral, Happy, Contentment, Challenge, Self-Esteem

Red Zone

**Anger, Fear, Anxiety, Hatred, Blame, Denial,
Sadness, Shame, Powerlessness**

Reflection and Discussion Questions:

a. Where have you been in the chart today or right now...the *Red, Green* or *Blue Zones?*

b. How much of the time are you in these different zones?

c. What emotions do you most frequently experience?

d. For homework, check in on where you are at every day. ...Are you mostly in Red, Green or Blue?

Session 2: I Know Me: Red Zone Emotions

Understanding your perception of yourself is another important aspect for creating awareness and stopping attachment, engagement, and participation in harmful cycles. Some reflection questions to consider on this...

Who do you see yourself as? Who do others perceive you as?
What words would you use to describe yourself, both 'positive' and 'negative'?

A big part of unhappiness is not knowing who we are and trying to be someone we are not or living a life that does not authentically suit us. This can easily cause situations where you may feel trapped in patterns, programs, and attachments for trying to be who you think you are 'supposed to be' and having no idea who you truly are. If you don't realize this is happening and learn to listen to your authentic self... an experience of hopelessness, depression, feelings of confusion, powerlessness, and even anger can occur. This week's materials are meant to be an introduction to better your understanding of who you are and who you are not. It is meant to encourage you to learn to listen to yourself and what best fits *your* life.

7 Days of Identity Insight: Complete the reflections below for each day, starting with Day 1.

a. What zone (red, green, or blue) do you tend to be in each day?

b. Where on the *Identity Layers Chart* are you today? "*What layer are you most affected by?*"

c. Where on the *Trapped Cycle* are you today (#'s 1-6)?

Blue Zone

Love, Peace, Joy, Gratitude, Harmony, Empathy, Compassion

Green Zone

Safety, Neutral, Happy, Contentment, Challenge, Self-Esteem

Red Zone

Anger, Fear, Anxiety, Hatred, Blame, Denial, Sadness, Shame, Powerlessness

Session 3: Strong, Happy Me ☺

When an individual or group experiences trauma, severe stress, violence, powerlessness, hopelessness or other things similar to this...it is not unusual to struggle with self-worth and self-confidence. In fact, survivors of trauma or abuse often suffer from lower self-esteem, negative, depressive thought patterns and blaming themselves for what they have experienced. This can be a way to cope with and try to make sense of things that are beyond our understanding. However, ultimately, negativity towards the self, negative thought patterns or beliefs, and staying in the victim or weakened mindset, only makes things worse in the end.

Our ability to foster and support a positive, resilient self is essential for strengthening ourselves to handle difficult, or traumatic life circumstances. No matter what the situation is, we can shift our mindset or perspective to help us become stronger and more empowered. The exercises covered in this session include the Emotion Chart Exercise, The Positive Identity Layers Exercise and The Nervous System, Safety & Rest Exercise.

The Emotion Chart Exercise is meant to help foster an awareness and comprehension for what emotions you are experiencing and the main zones you are living in, if these are the red, green or blue zones or some combination. The Positive Identity Layers Exercise is meant to help identity and reflect on what beliefs or thoughts you hold about yourself, your community and situation. It is an opportunity to reflect on how you view yourself, your community and environment and any beliefs you'd like to keep or change to better empower yourself. A positive identity is very powerful for resiliency and optimism in your own strengths and abilities, and ability to manage traumatic and high stress situations. The way we view ourselves, others and our community are powerful for how we navigate unknown or traumatic life circumstances and getting beyond them.

The Nervous System, Safety & Rest Exercise is the last exercise in this session and is also significant in its ability to foster and support greater inner strength, resiliency and healing. Trauma and severe stress due to humanitarian situations and disasters can be very hard on the nervous system and our daily living. It can negatively impact our thinking, mindset, ability to rebuild or navigate challenging circumstances, thrive, be successful and heal. By calming the nervous system, we can experience greater restoration, healing and even post-traumatic growth after severely stressful and painful life situations. It is recommended to do this exercise or a similar one every day to help calm the mind, body and nervous system, no matter what the circumstances may be.

First Exercise:

1. ***Emotion Chart Exercise*** *(approximately 15 minutes):*

Blue Zone
Love, Peace, Joy, Gratitude, Harmony, Empathy, Compassion
Green Zone
Safety, Neutral, Happy, Contentment, Challenge, Self-Esteem
Red Zone
Anger, Fear, Anxiety, Hatred, Blame, Denial, Sadness, Shame, Powerlessness

Reflection and Discussion Questions:

a. Where have you been in the chart today or right now…the *Red, Green* and/or *Blue Zones?*

b. How much are you in these different zones?

c. What is a "Blue or Green Zone" emotion you'd like to experience more of? How can you do 5 minutes a day of something small to bring this experience into your life?

Second Exercise:

2. *The Positive Identity Layers Exercise (approximately 20 minutes):*

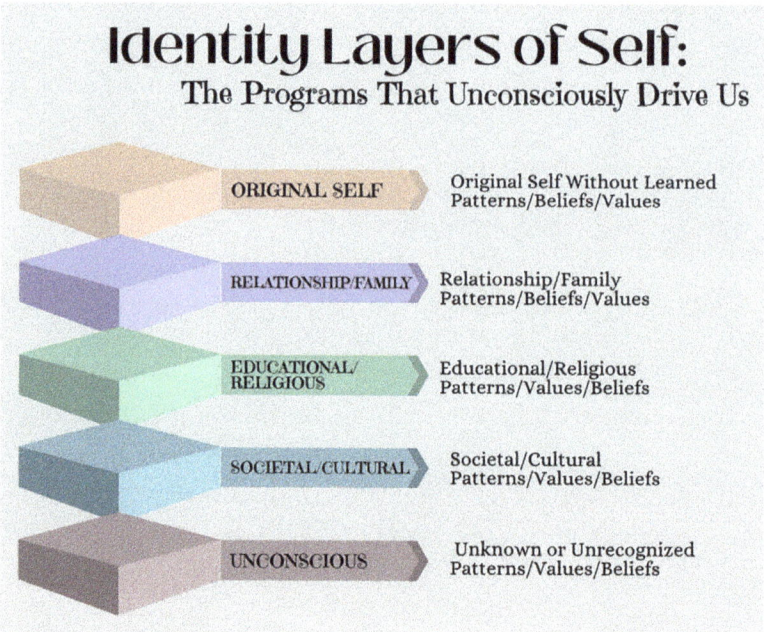

Reflection and Discussion Questions:

a. What are some patterns, values, or beliefs you hold about yourself that are positive?

b. What are some patterns, values or beliefs you hold about your family and close friends that are positive?

c. What are some patterns, values or beliefs you hold about your community that are positive?

d. Are there any patterns, values or beliefs you would like to have and add to your life that are positive?

Third Exercise:

3. *The Nervous System, Safety & Rest Exercise*
(approximately 15 minutes):

Close your eyes and sit in a comfortable position, and maybe with your feet on the floor
Take a deep breath in through your nose and out through your mouth
Take another deep breath in through your nose and out through your mouth
Take one more deep breath in through your nose and out through your mouth

And as I count down from 5 to 1, feeling more and more relaxed, calm and at peace
5 to 4 feeling more relaxed
4 to 3
3 to 2 calmer and calmer
2 to 1 feeling calm, relaxed and at peace

Imagine that you are sitting near a grassy green field and peaceful forest
Breath in peace and calm
Breath out the feeling of support and safety
Notice the breath in and out and the flow of the air

Now, imagine you are standing up and then are walking towards the forest
As you walk towards the forest, you feel more and more supported, calm and at peace
Deep breath in and out, allowing yourself in this moment to be safe and supported
Breathing in support and compassion
Breathing out support and compassion

Then imagine that you are wearing a back-pack full of rocks, and these rocks are everything and anything that is weighing you down, causing you trauma, stress, pain and fear
You walk over to a lake in the forest, and this lake dissolves any and all the rocks in your backpack
One by one throwing these rocks into the lake, and they melt and dissolve away

3

2

And 1

These rocks melt and dissolve away completely

And throwing your backpack into the lake now, and it dissolves away completely

And you feel lighter and lighter, more and more at peace and at ease

Deep breath in and out,

Imagining yourself sitting in this forest by the lake

And you are filled with rest

Your head, neck and shoulders…in this moment, you feel kindness and compassion foryourself

Your arms and hands ….in this moment, your arms and hands are filled with compassion and self-kindness

Your torso, heart, chest, and stomach…kindness and compassion

Your back, hips, legs and feet…all filled with kindness and compassion

And you breathe in a feeling of compassion, and breath out

Knowing that in this moment, you are filled with compassion, love and feel at peace…

Session 4: Happy Me ☺

In this session, we look at our innate ability and the application of certain practices that can help bring greater freedom from suffering. There is a balance between validating and honoring our experiences, and being free from the pain of them, so we can thrive and somehow improve our situations. Part of overcoming suffering from traumatic life events or chronic toxic stress is to honor and validate what you have experienced and have compassion for yourself and your suffering. Even if what you experienced is considered 'normal' in your community, family or society, it doesn't mean it didn't have a negative, painful impact. It doesn't mean things weren't done that were wrong or extremely harmful. However, normalizing or ignoring that pain and the experiences unfortunately will not make it go away. In fact, it can create harmful coping mechanisms or patterns that do not help you thrive and overcome and create issues like panic, severe anxiety, trauma symptoms, depression, hopelessness and even suicidal ideation. However, if we become extremely focused on our pain and suffering and what we have experienced, and it even becomes part of our identity, that is also problematic. There is a balance and middle way to manage extreme suffering or trauma so it does not consume or define you or your life in the long-term. The things that have happened in your life, the experiences you've had, and your current life situation doesn't have to be the end of your story or your identity. We can find a way to turn it into motivation for change, rebuilding and growth.

In this session we work on three exercises. The first is the Honor Your Suffering Exercise. In this, we work to validate and honor what we, others or our community has experienced that has created trauma and great pain. The goal is not to become stuck in the pain, but rather to honor and acknowledge it for the power it has and our own unique experience of it. Then to apply compassion to the pain and ourself.

The second exercise in this session is the Adapted Rational Emotive Behavior Therapy (REBT) Exercise. This is an opportunity to learn a tangible skill to help transform negative thoughts, feelings or beliefs into alternative, positive ones. The goal of this exercise is to provide information on a tangible skill that can be applied on a daily basis independently even after the session is done. The more you practice this activity, the more it becomes part of your everyday mindset and will help you manage stress, negative emotions and future events. The third exercise is the Blue Zone Emotion Chart Exercise. This is adapted from the Emotion Chart Exercise conducted in the first and second sessions. The goal of this activity is to cultivate greater focus on positive, 'blue zone' emotions and bring greater awareness to these emotions. By practicing noticing when you are having those emotions, and intentionally trying to create moments where you feel blue zone emotions, you create more neuropathways in the brain that allow for more blue zone thoughts and feelings. You also start to intentionally create more goodness in your life, even if it's just a small shift every day, or 1% happier every day or every week. Over time this adds up, when we intentionally try to focus on experiencing a few moments in the Blue Zone.

First Exercise:

1. ***Name Your Pain Exercise*** *(approximately 20 minutes):*

a. Please list at least 5 things that are upsetting you or 5 emotions you are struggling with such as guilt, anxiety, helplessness, powerlessness, overwhelm, sadness, fear, depression, stress, or shame.

b. Please discuss or write for 10 minutes on at least one of these 5 things

c. Then please reflect on compassion for these five things

Second Exercise:

2. ***Change Your Pain Exercise*** *(approximately 20 minutes):*

a. Please reflect on a negative thought or belief you have

b. Please discuss or write how this negative thought or belief may benefit you (usually it is a protective reason)

c. Please discuss or write how this negative thought or belief may harm you (usually it worsens life situation or negative emotions and puts you more in the 'Red Zone')

d. Please discuss or write at least 3 positive alternatives to this negative thought or belief

1) Negative Identified Belief:

What is the benefit of this negative identified belief?

What is the harm of this negative identified belief?

3 Positive Alternatives to Identified Belief:

a.

b.

c.

Third Exercise:

3. ***Blue Zone Emotion Chart Exercise*** *(approximately 10 minutes):*

a. Please look at the Blue Zone area of the chart below.

b. Are there any moments you experienced in the blue zone, even if it was 1 minute or less recently?

c. What blue zone emotion did you experience and why?

d. Can you try to create more blue zone emotions every day? If yes, which emotion would you like to try to focus on?

Uplifting and Lighening Emotions
Bliss, Serenity, Peace, Harmony, Self-Awareness, Balance
Joy, Enthusiasm, Abundance, Exhilaration, Hope
Compassion, Empathy, Inspiration, Clarity, Presence
Love, Appreciation, Gratitude, Devotion, Generosity

Session 5: Kind, Compassionate Me

First Exercise:

1. *The Compassion-Based Resiliency Exercise:*

Reflection and Discussion Questions:

a. What does *compassion* mean for you?

b. What does *compassion for others* mean?

c. When are some moments you have experienced some level of compassion? What did it feel like?

Compassion-Based Resiliency Chart

Full, Unconditional Compassion to Self and Others
Full Compassion to Self and Others
Partial Compassion to Self and Others
Neutral on Compassion to Self and Others
Partial Negative Judgement of Self and Others
Full Negative Judgement of Self and Others
Don't Understand or Know What This Means
Unconscious Reactions, Habits and Patterns

Second Exercise:

2. *7 Days of Kindness:*

Reflection and Discussion Questions:

a.   What is an act of kindness?

   b. Please intentionally do one act of kindness for yourself or someone else today.

Third Exercise:

3. *Gratitude/Manifestation and Fear Exercise:*

Reflection and Discussion Questions:
   1) Today what are you feeling thankful for?

   2) Today what are you having fear about?

Example:

Gratitude/Manifested Gratitude: I am so happy and thankful today because I have my summer vacation soon!

My Fears: I am afraid I will get bad grades before my summer vacation comes

Fourth Exercise:

4. *The Nervous System, Safety & Rest Exercise*
   (approximately 15 minutes):

Close your eyes and sit in a comfortable position, and maybe with your feet on the floor
Take a deep breath in through your nose and out through your mouth
Take another deep breath in through your nose and out through your mouth
Take one more deep breath in through your nose and out through your mouth

As I count down from 5 to 1, feeling more and more relaxed, calm, and at peace
5 to 4 feeling more relaxed
4 to 3
3 to 2 calmer and calmer
2 to 1 feeling calm, relaxed and at peace

Imagine that you are sitting near a grassy green field and a peaceful forest
Breathe in peace and calm
Breathe out the feeling of support and safety
Notice the breath in and out and the flow of the air

Now, imagine you are standing up and then walking towards the forest
As you walk toward the forest, you feel more and more supported, calm, and at peace
Deep breath in and out, allowing yourself in this moment to be safe and supported
Breathing in support and compassion
Breathing out support and compassion

Then imagine that you are wearing a backpack full of rocks, and these rocks are everything and anything that is weighing you down, causing you trauma, stress, pain, and fear
You walk over to a lake in the forest, and this lake dissolves all the rocks in your backpack
One by one throw these rocks into the lake, and they melt and dissolve away
3
2
And 1
These rocks melt and dissolve away completely
And throwing your backpack into the lake now, and it dissolves away completely
And you feel lighter and lighter, more and more at peace and ease

Deep breath in and out,
Imagining yourself sitting in this forest by the lake
And you are filled with rest

Your head, neck, and shoulders…in this moment, it is safe to rest
Your arms and hands ….in this moment, it is safe to rest
Your torso, heart, chest, and stomach…rest
Your back, hips, legs, and feet…all rest

And you breathe in a feeling of rest and breathe out
Knowing that at this moment, it is safe to rest, relax, and experience some peace…

Session 6: Precious Me ☺

A major component of well-being is love. Love can refer to kindness to others, kindness to yourself, friendship love, familial love, romantic love, love for humanity, and more. It can adapt and take so many forms and applications. So how do we put this into practice? How do we put this into action? In this week and next, we will cover tangible exercises to improve and better understand the experience of love in your life. Love is a huge transformer of negative emotions and circumstances into positive, uplifting experiences. Love opens and connects, while fear tends to shut down and close off. Some practices that help us to increase our experience of love, peace, and contentment include the gratitude manifestation and fear exercise, as well as the self-love and other-love awareness exercises.

What does love mean to you? Do you feel it's referring to only romantic, friendship, or familial love? What if it's a larger, encompassing life force energy that makes up and manifests all that exists? What if by focusing on love, you are opening yourself up to feeling happier than you've ever been before?

First Exercise:

1. *Self-Love Chart Exercise:*

Reflection and Discussion Questions:

a. What does: 1) self-love, 2) self-like, 3) self-dislike, and 4) self-hatred mean to you?

b. Where are you in the 'Self-Love' Chart? :)

Love Myself Unconditionally
Love Myself
Like Myself
Neutral about Myself
Don't Like Myself
Hate Myself
Don't Understand or Know What This Means
Unconscious Reactions, Habits, and Patterns

Second Exercise:

2. *Other-Love Chart Exercise:*

Reflection and Discussion Questions:

a. What does: 1) other-love, 2) other-like, 3) other-dislike, and 4) other-hatred mean to you?

b. Where are you in the 'Other-Love' Chart? :)

Love Others Unconditionally
Love Others
Like Others
Neutral about Others
Don't Like Others
Hate Others
Don't Understand or Know What This Means
Unconscious Reactions, Habits, and Patterns

Third Exercise:

3. *You Are Valuable Exercise:*

You are special, precious, and unique just as you are. You were born with innate value and worth that is unconditional, and you have no matter what has happened to you and no matter what someone says or does.

    a. What is something that has made you feel you are less valuable orworthy? Have you ever felt 'less than' because of something that hashappened or been said to you?

    b. What are times when you knew without a doubt, that you were valuable,loved, and loveable?

For Instructors of the Youth-Focused HBM:

1. Participate in all 3 sessions with a certified Brief Trauma-Focused HBM instructor and review the program, core concepts, course set-up and activities.

2. Please complete the Brief Trauma-Focused HBM and all 3 sessions. By completing the program, it will help you to be ready to teach so you are familiar and have a deep understanding of the material.

3. Please read and reference all materials in the program and become familiar with the activities and the on-going practice of them. This includes a comfortable use and regular application of all activities provided.

www.ingramcontent.com/pod-product-compliance
Lightning Source LLC
Chambersburg PA
CBHW051139120626
46547CB00012B/866